MW00329378

"This world desperately needs to know the love, hope, and life that is only found in Jesus Christ. I believe this book is an outstanding resource that can help followers of Jesus make a dynamic gospel impact in their communities, this nation, and world!"

—**Dr. Brad Jurkovich, Senior Pastor, First Baptist Church, Bossier City, LA**

"The life and ministry of B. Gray Allison was defined by the wisdom of Proverbs 11:30, 'He who wins souls is wise.' His passion for personal evangelism was contagious, and his teaching was biblical, clear, and accessible. This collection of his work is a treasure, and I am thankful it will be passed on to future generations of readers and students."

—**Josh Reavis, Associate Pastor, North Jax Baptist Church**

"Thank you, Dr. Spradlin, for bringing to life Dr. Gray Allison's personal evangelism lectures. Reading them evoked wonderful memories sitting in his classes. One could not sit in Dr. Gray's class without being stirred to action. Embedded in my memory are his words, 'God help me see in those I meet on country road and city street, not just people passing by, but those for whom Jesus came to die.'"

—**Dr. Bob Pearle, Senior Pastor, Birchman Baptist Church**

"Dr B. Gray Allison's heart for souls is on display throughout his classroom notes. As a student I heard Dr Gray say, 'If you share Christ with enough people, someone will be saved. When that happens, God will "set your shucks on fire." You will never be the same.' He was a man who carried a fire for missions and evangelism and touched a generation. I know because he touched my life."

—**Dr. Monte Shinkle, Senior Pastor, Concord Baptist Church, MABTS Alumnus: MDIV 1980, DMIN 1994**

PERSONAL EVANGELISM

B. GRAY ALLISON, PhD
EDITED AND REVISED BY MICHAEL R. SPRADLIN, PhD

innovo PUBLISHING

Published by Innovo Publishing, LLC
www.innovopublishing.com
1-888-546-2111

Providing Full-Service Publishing Services for Christian Authors, Artists & Ministries: Hardbacks, Paperbacks, eBooks, Audiobooks, Music, Screenplays & Curricula

PERSONAL EVANGELISM

Copyright © 2021 by Michael R. Spradlin
All rights reserved.

No part of this publication may be reproduced, stored in a retrieval system, or transmitted in any form or by any means electronic, mechanical, photocopying, recording, or otherwise, without the prior written permission of the author.

Scripture marked "NASB" was taken from the New American Standard Bible, copyright © 1960, 1962, 1963, 1968, 1971, 1972, 1973, 1975, 1977, 1995 by The Lockman Foundation

Scripture marked "KJV" was taken from the King James Version of the Bible. Public domain.

Scripture marked "RSV" was taken from the Revised Standard Version of the Bible, copyright © 1946, 1952, and 1971 the Division of Christian Education of the National Council of the Churches of Christ in the United States of America. Used by permission. All rights reserved.

Contributors: Thomas Hammond, Executive Director of the Georgia Baptist Convention; and Dr. Brad Roderick, Professor of Missions, Mid-America Baptist Theological Seminary and Retired Missionary with the International Mission Board of the Southern Baptist Convention

Library of Congress Control Number: 2021930761
ISBN: 978-1-61314-624-8

Cover Design & Interior Layout: Innovo Publishing, LLC

Printed in the United States of America
U.S. Printing History
First Edition: 2021

Dedicated to Pastor Ed Edmondson, who led me to Christ and showed me how to be a soul winner, and to Dr. B. Gray Allison, who fanned the flames of evangelism.

ACKNOWLEDGMENTS

Thank you to Cary Beth Duffel, Executive Assistant to the President, for her tireless efforts in bringing this manuscript to fruition.

Special thanks to Taffey Hall of the Southern Baptist Historical Library and Archives for finding several articles on evangelism that Dr. Allison wrote for Southern Baptist publications through the years.

Editor Rachael Carrington has done a tremendous job in preparing the manuscript. This is the fourth book we have worked on together.

CONTENTS

B. GRAY ALLISON BIOGRAPHY

Img. 1: Gray and Voncille Allison

Born on May 7, 1924, Gray Allison came from a strong Christian home and a large family. He was the eighth of ten children born to John Richard Preston "Buddy" Allison and Ora Byram Allison. Gray credited his mother with his love of learning and his love of the Bible. As a young man, he was one of eleven people saved in a revival meeting in the small town of Ida, Louisiana. That revival meeting saw a total of eleven converts baptized into the membership of the Ida Baptist Church August 14, 1935, by Pastor John H. Haldeman in Ben Mean's cow pond. After the baptism, the congregation sang the hymn, "O Happy Day." Gray matured physically and in his faith, but the advent of the second world war interrupted his college studies and put him on a new path in life.

While in the Pacific serving as a pilot in the Army Air Forces, Gray continued to sense a call to the ministry. He set the call aside, and after the war, he went into business selling insurance. He eventually surrendered to the call to ministry and enrolled in New Orleans Baptist Theological Seminary (NOBTS). By 1952 he was married and pastoring two part-time churches in Northern Louisiana. While in seminary, Gray was greatly influenced by the avid soul winner and president of the NOBTS, Roland Q. Leavell. Previously, Dr. Leavell had served in the evangelism department of the Home Mission Board of the Southern Baptist Convention (SBC) and brought his passion for evangelism with him to NOBTS.

By the time Gray Allison graduated with his doctorate from seminary (his second seminary degree), he was so well respected that he was asked to join the faculty of NOBTS as a professor of missions and the director of the school's signature Practical Missions program. This program required students to share the gospel regularly with the Word of God in a genuine attempt to lead a lost person to Christ.

After several years as a seminary professor, Dr. Allison would go on to serve with the Home Mission Board of the Southern Baptist Convention with the task of increasing evangelism on college and seminary campuses. At one time, Gray believed that the Lord was calling him to be a missionary in South Korea, but the Lord never confirmed that call. Even so, Dr. Allison maintained a life-long passion for South Korea from that time onward. Later, he would form and lead the Allison Evangelistic Association and preach revivals across the United States and around the world.

Img. 2: Gray Allison in South Korea where he thought the Lord might want him to serve as a missionary.

After years of praying with close friends and associates for a seminary to recapture the passion for the Bible, missions, and evangelism, it was decided that a new seminary was needed to train pastors with these key passions. Though the formation of a new seminary severed many friendships for Dr. Gray (as he came to be called by his students), Mid-America Baptist Theological Seminary (MABTS) was launched in 1972. The school was built on the three emphases of the Bible as the inerrant Word of God, missions as the call on every believer's life, and personal evangelism as the practice of every New Testament Christian. The seminary started in Little Rock, Arkansas, but eventually moved to Memphis, Tennessee, in 1975 where it continues to this day.

Part of Dr. Allison's legacy was to bring the Practical Missions program with him to the new seminary. Every seminary student has been, and still is, required to share the gospel on a weekly basis with the Word of God in a genuine attempt to lead a lost person to Christ. Almost every graduate of MABTS was personally instructed in evangelism by Dr. Gray, and this book contains many of the notes he used through the years to train thousands of pastors, church staff leaders, and missionaries in personal evangelism. Dr. Gray never felt that his method was the only way to reach people for Christ, but he strongly believed that the fire and passion for evangelism could be passed on—"caught" as it were—to every student and then on to the churches where they served.[1]

In addition to his years teaching missions and evangelism at New Orleans Baptist Theological Seminary, Gray Allison taught personal evangelism at Mid-America Baptist Theological Seminary from 1972 until 2017, two

Img. 3: Gray Allison in South Korea, one of the many countries where he preached and ministered.

years before his death in 2019, an evangelistic teaching ministry of well over fifty years at the two schools. Ed Edmondson, the pastor that led me to Christ, the editor of this work, was taught personal evangelism by Gray Allison while a student at New Orleans Baptist Theological Seminary.

PREFACE

The genesis of this work was the need for a textbook for the class on personal evangelism at Mid-America Baptist Theological Seminary. Dr. Allison taught this signature class for almost forty-seven years and used his own notes supplemented by other readings from numerous sources. The combination of Allison's unique approach (it's not a method but a lifelong practice) and the dearth of current materials on personal evangelism prompted this book's creation. The intent of the book is to capture Dr. Gray Allison's philosophy to teach future students the practice of personal evangelism.

With the exception of one academic year, when Dr. C. E. Autrey taught personal evangelism, every Mid-America student through the years studied evangelism under the tutelage of Gray Allison. During Dr. Allison's tenure, Mid-America had a residential campus in both Memphis, Tennessee, and in Colonie (Albany), New York. Although Dr. Allison did not personally teach evangelism to the New York students, every New York campus professor that taught evangelism there was one of his former students. Even new Mid-America faculty members who were not Mid-America graduates would often audit Gray Allison's classes so that they could learn evangelism from him personally and directly.

For decades, graduates of Allison's evangelism classes graduated from seminary and went out to teach evangelism in their local churches and on mission fields around the world. With the addition of graduates that taught in other seminaries worldwide, it would be difficult to calculate the impact on personal evangelism that Gray Allison had for untold thousands and tens of thousands of believers in Christ. In addition to this, the number of people who prayed to receive Christ while Mid-America students numbered well over one hundred thousand while Dr. Allison was the seminary's president. The number of people who prayed to receive Christ through the witness of a Mid-America graduate or even through the student of a Mid-America graduate would be incalculable. The methods espoused by Allison's work and have been proven in numerous places and through the years.

All undocumented quotes in this book come from various editions of Gray Allison's unpublished class notes. When possible, sources have been cited, but in some cases no reference was provided in his personal notes and no source could be clearly identified. Statistics used in Dr. Allison's notes were current at the time of his writing. These statistics have not been updated, but they will still serve their intended purpose—to illustrate the spiritually lost condition of the world. Other items mentioned in the text come from the editor's personal interaction with Dr. Allison over the course of three decades of ministry together.

All Scripture quotations are marked in the text, and most of the references come either from the New American Standard Bible (1995 edition) or the King James Version. Typically, the King James Version translation was used by Dr. Allison in his notes, and updated sections of the book will use the 1995 edition of the New American Standard Bible translation. The translation used is always noted in the text unless the translation was Dr. Allison's personal translation of the Greek New Testament.

CHAPTER 1

INTRODUCTION TO PERSONAL EVANGELISM

Evangelism is more caught than taught. (Dr. B. Gray Allison)

1.A. THE APPROACH TO TEACHING EVANGELISM

This book intends to motivate believers in Jesus Christ to practice biblical obedience to Him by sharing their faith with unbelievers on a regular basis. The plan of the book is to inform, motivate, train, and do personal evangelism.

Every generation of believers must make their own decision about a commitment to personal evangelism. Methods and terminology frequently change, but certain biblical core essentials must be in place. This question must be answered by every born-again believer in Jesus Christ: Will I love my neighbor by telling them the news of Christ's death, burial, and resurrection on the cross and how that impacts their life?

Citing statistics of the crisis for the current generation may assist in short-term motivation, but only an understanding of the biblical commands and imperatives will have a lasting effect on turning a believer into a multiplier—that is, a Great-Commission Christian.

The philosophy of Gray Allison in teaching evangelism will be used throughout this book. That philosophy could almost be called "biblical evangelism" because of his emphasis on making the Scriptures the centerpiece of each witnessing encounter.

Dr. Allison practiced what he preached about personal evangelism in that he was a regular witness for Christ. He would share in chapel at Mid-America Seminary on a weekly basis about the people he had shared the gospel with that week. His wife, Voncille, and their daughters and son were also active witnesses in their own lives. Dr. Gray would challenge his students to try and catch him without his soul-winner's New Testament. If they were successful, then he would buy them a steak dinner. Only one student that I am aware of ever successfully claimed that promise.

Another overlooked aspect of Gray Allison's view of evangelism was his focus on making the Bible the centerpiece in evangelism. Allison believed that the Word of God was the key to the evangelistic message. He did not develop an outline and then attach a few key verses; he saturated each witnessing encounter with the Bible. He even made a comment in class that if someone would not listen to the Bible, then he did not know how to witness to them.

Finally, because of Dr. Allison's extensive evangelism ministry, even after he became a seminary president, he understood the needs of local churches and gained wisdom from local church pastors. After World War II, when the Southern Baptist Convention became a juggernaut for missions and evangelism, Gray Allison was a part of this movement and personally knew most of the principle leaders in the SBC missions and evangelism movement. Allison's extensive number of local church revivals meant that he talked with some of the best soul-winning pastors in the world on a regular basis. His approach was not born out of academia but from the battleground of the local church where, as Allison commented, pastors had to wrestle with the devil, evil, and sin on a regular basis. Evangelism was not a theoretical exercise but a desperate rescue mission to the lost and dying sinners of the world.

1.B. FROM THEOLOGY TO PRACTICE

Some have tried to tie the necessity for evangelism to the promise given to Abraham in Genesis 12:1-3 (NASB). When God promises that "in you all the families of the earth will be blessed," He is promising the coming of Jesus as the Messiah. While the Old Testament is saturated with Jesus on every page, the clearest starting point for evangelism is the Great Commission as outlined in each of the four Gospels.

In looking at Matthew 28:16-20, the resurrected Lord Jesus appears, giving His personal instruction to His closest followers. Despite their doubts (or possibly because of them) the followers of Jesus are commanded (not just advised) to (1) go; (2) make disciples (believers, followers); (3) baptize these very followers; and (4) teach them to obey all things.

The Great Commission is repeated in all four Gospels. In fact, the Great Commission passage is a great argument that the long ending of Mark is inspired, since, without it, the Gospel of Mark would be the only Gospel without the Great Commission.

Evangelism, winning people to a saving relationship with the Lord Jesus, is the heart of God's purpose, plan, and program for every local New Testament church. To understand the Bible rightly, as long as we are here on this earth, until Jesus comes again, the top priority of any and every church is evangelism. Everything a church does should relate to winning people to Christ.

Personal evangelism has always had its critics. Some have argued that a local church should focus on quality growth versus quantity growth. A prospective seminary student once told the editor of this work that his church focused on discipleship and did not do evangelism because of the abuse of personal evangelism. This wrong evangelism had allowed many church members to believe that they were saved but were not. I asked if his church's goal was to have fewer, better quality people in heaven? How can a church be obedient to Scripture and not practice evangelism? How can a discipleship program be biblical if it does not include personal evangelism?

Another objection to the practice of personal evangelism emphasizes the teaching of the Great Commandment as opposed to the Great Commission. This idea is that believers are required to love others above all else. In response to this, it must be pointed out that any Christian activity that will allow a lost person to go to hell without the Gospel is not a loving activity.

A further objection to personal evangelism is that the gift of evangelism is only given to a small percentage of church members. The majority of church members, without the gift of evangelism, should not do evangelism because they are not gifted for it by the Holy Spirit. This view falls apart when examined next to Scripture. No gift of evangelism is present in the New Testament (though evangelists are listed as a gift to a church (Ephesians 4:11). Yet, the Scriptures are consistent and clear in their commands to do evangelism.

No objection changes the fact that evangelism is the most wonderful work in the world. It is the most God-honoring work on this earth. Finally, considering the consequences of a soul dying without Jesus, it is the most urgently needed work in the world.

After looking at the biblical basis and motivation for evangelism, a clear definition of what evangelism is must be established. If your definition of evangelism is weak, then your plans for and performance of the work of evangelism will be limited by a lack of clarity and dedication.

1.C. A BRIEF BIBLICAL SURVEY OF EVANGELISM

Does the concept of evangelism exist in the Old Testament? This is a valid question of biblical interpretation to ask. Can an argument for sharing one's faith be made using the Old Testament Scriptures?

Could one difference in the testaments be that the New Testament ushered in a "missionary" age as well as the preaching of grace through faith? Did the Old Testament faithful have any obligation to "spread the news" of their God? One verse commonly used in motivating New Testament believers to witness is found in Proverbs 11:30 (KJV): "He that winneth souls is wise." Since this is an Old Testament reference, were the Old Testament saints expected to be soul winners?

1.C.1. EVANGELISM IN THE OLD TESTAMENT

Making decisions, which can be called *decisionism*, is found in the Old Testament. Since the New Testament and Old Testament are not opposites but parts of one Bible inspired by God the Holy Spirit, it should be no surprise that common concepts exist between the two testaments. The next section will identify key passages that either talk about a "faith event" or show an example of an Old Testament figure calling for a spiritual decision to follow the Lord.[2]

The Old Testament comes complete with "faith events." Hebrews 11 examines the lives of Old Testament heroes and states that "faith" was a part of their becoming righteous. From Abel to Moses, these events of faith are highlighted by the author of Hebrews (whom this editor believes to be the Apostle Paul; Dr. Allison believed that the author of Hebrews may have been the New Testament person Apollos). In addition to these "faith events," proper names were changed (for example: Jacob to Israel, Genesis 32:28) and Old Testament saints "called" upon the name of the Lord (Genesis 4:26). These events imply a spiritual dynamic that should be examined.

In Exodus 32:26 (KJV), Moses spoke to the Israelites and said, "Who is on the Lord's side? Let him come unto me." And in verse 29, Moses said, "Consecrate yourselves today to the Lord, even every man upon his son, and upon his brother; that he may bestow upon you a blessing this day." In each of these instances, Moses is calling for an immediate decision and that decision is to make a commitment to the Lord.

While Joshua was making one of his final addresses to the Israelites, he said, "And if it seem evil unto you to serve the Lord, choose you this day whom ye will serve; whether the gods which your fathers served that were on the other side of the flood, or the gods of the Amorites, in whose land ye dwell: but as for me and my house, we will serve the Lord" (Joshua 24:15 KJV). Once again, a clear call to make a divine choice is indicated. Further, a time-specific decision is requested.

"And Elijah came unto all the people, and said, 'How long halt ye between two opinions? if the Lord be God, follow him: but if Baal, then follow him'" (1 Kings 18:21 KJV). A call for a choice between gods is made, and the invitation includes the choice of a god and the intent to follow the god that is chosen. Furthermore, Elijah intends for the choice to be the Lord and not Baal.

The prophet Amos issued a concise and clear call to follow the Lord. His instructions were to "Seek good, and not evil, that ye may live: and so the LORD, the God of hosts, shall be with you, as ye have spoken" (Amos 5:14 KJV). The invitation of Amos not only called for a decision, but it included the benefit of a right decision. The benefit that Amos included was "life."

Jeremiah gave instructions on how to make a divine decision by his words in chapter 33 verse 3 (KJV): "Call unto me, and I will answer thee, and show thee great and mighty things, which thou knowest not." This invitation included two promises. One promise was that the calling would be answered, and the other promise was that action would result from the calling.

In 1 Samuel 10:5 (KJV), a reference is made to "a company of prophets." While conclusions would be difficult to draw based on the limited information in Scripture, a "school of the prophets" seemed to exist in the Old Testament period. It could easily be inferred that any prophetic ministry in Israel would be to promote the proper worship of the Lord. These prophets would call for a decision to leave idolatry and follow the Lord.

Solomon, in Ecclesiastes 12:1 (KJV), says, "Remember now thy Creator in the days of thy youth, while the evil days come not, nor the years draw nigh, when thou shalt say, 'I have no pleasure in them.'" Based on a lifetime of experience, Solomon extends an invitation to choose God. Embedded within this invitation is a warning of the result of a life not spent in the service of the Lord.

Now that it is established that divine decisions were called for in the Old Testament, three questions remain to be answered. Question (1): Is Proverbs 11:30 (KJV) really about soul winning? Question (2): Was a faith event necessary for salvation in the Old Testament? Question (3): Were all native-born Israelites followers of the LORD?

(1) If "soul winning" refers to a change of spiritual direction, then Proverbs 11:30 is a valid verse to be used to encourage New Testament soul winning. God's plan has always included reconciling sinners unto Himself, and the verse well fits into that context. (2) The Old Testament followers of the Lord were required to have a "faith event" to be right with the Lord. Abram called upon the Lord and became Abraham. Jacob called upon the Lord and became Israel. Surely the change of their personal names represents more than just a divine preference for a different nomenclature. (3) This point is further clarified with the understanding that not all of the ancient Israelites were faithful followers of the Lord. The need to destroy alternative places of worship and the prophetic

condemnations of idolatry show that some Israelites had not embraced the Lord as their God.

A call for life-changing decisions in the Old Testament was a normal part of the Israelite faith. The prophets constantly called for decisions that resulted in changed lives. New Testament evangelism also called for a decision, a decision to trust Jesus Christ as Lord and Savior.

The Old Testament had messengers with the message of the coming Messiah. These messengers were to tell Israel and the nations their message. The message called for a divine decision: "Will you follow the Lord?" Old Testament evangelism was, therefore, biblical evangelism.

1.C.2. EVANGELISM IN THE NEW TESTAMENT

The New Testament foundation of biblical evangelism is two-fold. First comes the message of Jesus, the Messiah, the Lord, and the Savior. Second comes the message calling people to surrender, repent, and follow this same Jesus. The ministry of the Lord Jesus was not to bring people information to better their lives; it was to bring people to Him in a personal, saving relationship. Once a person accepted the Lord Jesus as their Savior, they then had a mission to bring others to this same Jesus. The Lord Jesus said, "Follow Me, and I will make you fishers of men" (Matthew 4:19 NASB). So every part of the work and ministry of Jesus was endued with purpose. He came to die on the cross for sin and rise again victorious from the dead. He came to transform lives with the power of the gospel. He came to turn sinners into evangelists. He came to change the world.

Each of the four Gospels contains a section that has come to be called the Great Commission. The Great Commission serves as instructions for followers of Jesus to take His message to the nations. This commandment is repeated in each Gospel for emphasis and is an unbreakable command for believers in every age and culture.

Matthew 28:18-20 (NASB): And Jesus came up and spoke to them, saying, "All authority has been given to Me in heaven and on earth. Go therefore and make disciples of all the nations, baptizing them in the name of the Father and the Son and the Holy Ghost, teaching them to observe all that I commanded you; and lo, I am with you always, even to the end of the age."

Mark 16:15 (NASB): And He said to them, "Go into all the world and preach the gospel to all creation."

It should be noted that this editor believes that verses 9–20 in Mark 16 are Scripture and should be included in the text, in part, because they contain the Gospel of Mark's only Great Commission mandate.

> Luke 24:46-48 (NASB): And He said to them, "Thus it is written, that the Christ would suffer and rise again from the dead the third day, and that repentance for forgiveness of sins would be proclaimed in His name to all the nations, beginning from Jerusalem. You are witnesses of these things."

> John 20:21 (NASB): So Jesus said to them again, "Peace be with you; as the Father has sent Me, I also send you."

The book of Acts contains the blueprint for the missionary expansion of New Testament churches throughout the world. Acts 1:8 (NASB) says, "But you will receive power when the Holy Spirit has come upon you; and you shall be My witnesses both in Jerusalem, and in all Judea and Samaria, and even to the remotest part of the earth." More than just a geographical footprint of gospel transmission, this passage reiterates the need to take the gospel to all the world.

In a conference years ago, missionary Jim R. Sibley discussed this passage of Scripture with an insightful approach. Dr. Sibley explained the passage with a cultural contrasted with geographical examination of the passage. As Sibley explained, the audience of the Acts 1:8 text were the first Christians, who were mainly Jewish, and the center of Judaism was Jerusalem. So the first part of the command to take the gospel to Jerusalem could be understood as, "take the gospel to the people most like yourself." The second part of the commission in Acts is to take the gospel to Judea who would be ethnically and culturally Jewish, so take the gospel "to the people who are nearly like you." Samaria was an area populated in Jesus' day by people who were partly Jewish but were estranged from the Jewish people as a whole. The parable of the Good Samaritan illustrates that a "despised" person can be the hero of the story because the Samaritan helps his neighbor while the religious Jewish people do not help. This cultural conflict could make the passage mean to "take the Gospel to the people you do not like." Finally, the "remotest part of the earth" could be culturally translated to "take the gospel to the people you do not know."[3]

In the book of Acts, we see that the early Christians regularly and powerfully practiced their evangelism. The religious leaders of the New Testament era are quoted as "Saying, 'We gave you strict orders not to continue teaching in this name, and yet, you have filled Jerusalem with your teaching and intend to bring this man's blood upon us'" (Acts 5:28 NASB). Luke wrote further in Acts, "Therefore, those who had been scattered went about preaching the word"

(Acts 8:4 NASB). In Acts 13:26 (NASB) the Apostle Paul is recorded to have preached, "Brethren, sons of Abraham's family, and those among you who fear God, to us the message of this salvation has been sent."

The Apostle Paul wrote so much about the details of trusting Jesus that you can present the entire plan of salvation from just one of his books, the book of Romans. This approach is often called the Romans Road plan of salvation and is a favorite of Dr. Adrian Rogers, long time pastor of Bellevue Baptist Church in Memphis, Tennessee (see: Romans 3:10; 3:23; 5:1-2; 5:8; 6:23; 8:1; 10:9-10; and 10:13). Also, Paul clearly defined the gospel in 1 Corinthians 15:1-4 (NASB) when he stated, "Now I make known to you, brethren, the gospel which I preached to you, which also you received, in which also you stand, by which also you are saved, if you hold fast the word which I preached to you, unless you believed in vain. For I delivered to you as of first importance what I also received, that Christ died for our sins according to the Scriptures, and that He was buried, and that He was raised on the third day according to the Scriptures."

In 1 Corinthians 9:16-24 and 2 Corinthians 5:9-21, Paul shared his passion for telling everyone the good news of Jesus Christ. "Therefore, knowing the fear of the Lord, we persuade men, but we are made manifest to God" (2 Corinthians 5:11 NASB). The good news of the gospel deserves to be told to all that will listen.

So if the gospel of Jesus Christ is good news, and if the Bible commands us to go, why do so many who claim Christ never share their faith? Even our Lord Jesus lamented this fact in Matthew's Gospel. "Seeing the people, He felt compassion for them, because they were distressed and dispirited like sheep without a shepherd. Then He said to His disciples, 'The harvest is plentiful, but the workers are few. Therefore beseech the Lord of the harvest to send out workers into His harvest'" (Matthew 9:36-38 NASB). The conclusion is that a lack of evangelism comes from a lack of love for lost people, but most of all it is a prayer problem. We must pray that the Lord will send out more workers. Let us pray this very prayer each and every day of our lives.

CHAPTER 2

PREPARATION FOR PERSONAL EVANGELISM

2.A. EVANGELISM DEFINED

A comprehensive definition of evangelism is found in the numerous writings of an evangelism scholar from a previous generation, Dr. C. E. Autrey. Dr. Autrey wrote, "Evangelism is the outreach of the church into the world by confrontation with the Gospel of Christ in an attempt to lead people to a personal commitment in Christ by faith and repentance in Christ as Savior and Lord."[4]

Gray Allison described evangelism as "Christian intelligence on fire." He described it as more than an attempt to change moral and social conditions; more than an attempt to get people to attend church. It is the goal to see someone evangelized and discipled and serving the Lord through one of His churches.

No biblical divide exists between evangelism and discipleship. Evangelism that does not produce disciples of Jesus Christ is not biblical discipleship. Discipleship that does not produce evangelists for the Lord Jesus Christ is not the discipleship of the New Testament, where every believer was expected to be a witness for Christ.

2.B. PREPARING A NEW TESTAMENT FOR PERSONAL WITNESSING

Our purpose is to learn how to witness to other people with the written Word of God, in order to lead them to a knowledge of Jesus Christ as Lord and

Savior. We should say the written Word of God advisedly, because experience has shown that no substitute exists for witnessing with the written Word of God. One may learn Scripture, and every Christian should memorize Scripture. One may quote Scripture, and he may tell people of his own experience, but if one is really going to witness effectively to people and bring them to know Jesus as Lord, he must use the written Word of God. The Bible states of itself that the Word is the "sword of the Spirit" (Ephesians 6:17 NASB). It is the Word of God that pierces down to the deep places (Hebrews 4:12). It is the Word of God that the Spirit uses as a sword to bring conviction and to bring conversion (Romans 10:17).

So if we are witnessing, we need to give to the Holy Spirit the sword of the Spirit for His work. Now, it is a wonderful thing to share your experience in the Lord with other people, and that is a form of witnessing. But to be effective in witnessing, one needs to give them the Word of God. No person can convict another person of sin. The Holy Spirit brings conviction, and He does it through the Word of God. And no one has ever been saved until he was convicted of sin. So the believer is urged to use the written Word of God in witnessing. Though a believer may doubt that they can accomplish this, the Bible guarantees that you can do it. Not only can a believer do this, a believer must do this if you are to be an effective witness for the Lord. You will never be a truly joyful child of God until you are obedient. I know that you can do it, and I hope that you will do it. Use the written Word of God in witnessing.

In helping someone come to know Jesus, the first thing we have to show them is that they are a sinner in need of salvation. The Word of God tells them plainly, so that they cannot misunderstand it, that he is a sinner and that sin separates him from God. This shows him the necessity of salvation.

The second thing we want to show him is that salvation has been provided. We need to tell him what God has done for him and show him in the Word of God that God has done it.

The third thing we want to show him is how to be saved. These three are necessary if we are going to help people come to know the Lord. And so, in these lessons, we are going to talk about how to help people see that they are sinners who need to be saved, that God has provided for their salvation, and how they may be saved.

Gray Allison stated, "I would suggest to you, if you are going to be a real witness for the Lord, that you get a Bible or New Testament to use *just for witnessing*. I have a preaching Bible that I use just for preaching. I have Bibles that I use for study, but I have a little Testament, that I use for soul winning. That is my soul-winning Testament, and I use it only for soul winning."

Several advantages exist for having a New Testament to use for soul winning. (1) You can put marks in the Bible to note every passage that is relevant for soul winning. (2) When a New Testament is used just for soul winning, it will tend to open itself up to the right passage. One does not have to search for them anymore—the New Testament will tend to open itself up to the right places because it gets opened so many times to those verses. If you use this Bible or New Testament for devotional reading or study, or for preaching and teaching, this would not be true.

You should use a New Testament rather than a whole Bible for witnessing for several reasons. For one thing, this is enough of the Word of God to use in witnessing, and for another thing, it is convenient to carry in any pocket or bag.

You always need your marked New Testament with you because you never know when you are going to have an opportunity to witness to somebody, and you will need the sword of the Spirit with you. We are in a war with the devil, and we must have our weapon, the Word of God, to go into battle. The Word is the sword of the Spirit. You should carry it with you everywhere you go.

Dr. Gray shared this story:

Some time ago I was in a meeting in Jackson, Mississippi. I was leading a group of people who were interested in helping other folks to come to know the Lord. On Wednesday night, we marked our Testaments with the plan of salvation. One of the participants in the soul-winner's course was a public school teacher. On Thursday, at coffee time at school, she was showing the other teachers how she had marked the Testament and telling them about the soul-winner's course. As she went to her car that afternoon, intending to make a visit to someone she had on her heart, a sixth-grade teacher came to the door of the school, called her and asked if she would come back. When she did, the sixth grade teacher said, "Would you come and talk with me about how to be saved?" She went to the teacher's lounge, took out that little Testament she had marked just the night before, and had the privilege of leading a sixth-grade teacher to the Lord. She said that night when she came to church, "Oh, suppose I hadn't marked that Testament, or suppose I had not had it with me in my purse."

Get a New Testament or a Bible to use just for soul winning. It is worth it if you are serious about witnessing. You could do without something to buy a good New Testament, though you do not need an expensive Bible. Take the New Testament or Bible with you everywhere you go and never be without it because you never know when you will have an opportunity to tell somebody about the Lord.

CHAPTER 3

THE SOUL-WINNER'S MISSION

What is the soul-winner's mission in life? Jesus said, "As the Father has sent Me, I also send you" (John 20:21 NASB). This means that the mission is the same as that of Jesus in this world, and His mission is stated in Luke 4:18-19 (NASB). This was the beginning of the public ministry of Jesus when He said, "The Spirit of the LORD is upon Me, Because He anointed Me to preach the Gospel to the poor. He has sent Me to proclaim release to the captives, And recovery of sight to the blind, To set free those who are oppressed, To proclaim the favorable year of the LORD." Let us then examine His mission because it truly is our mission.[5]

3.A. PREACH GOOD TIDINGS TO THE POOR

This does not mean that Jesus came to preach good tidings to those without worldly possessions; rather, it means that Jesus came to preach the good news to those who are spiritually destitute. The expression "the poor" might really read, "to such as are poor." The word *tokos* means "to cringe" or "to crouch" like a beggar and is stronger than just "poor." In the Sermon on the Mount, Jesus calls them, "the beggarly poor in spirit" (Matthew 5:3 Allison translation). Isaiah 66:2 (NASB) says, "But to this one I will look, To him who is humble and contrite of spirit, and who trembles at My word." This attitude grows out of a person's realization of their utter helplessness and beggary, as far as personal ability or possession is concerned. Every unregenerate person is destitute spiritually. They are lost, damned, condemned, estranged from God, at enmity with God, spiritually naked, and without hope. It is to these people that Jesus came to preach the good news. This, then, is the mission of the soul winner.

3.B. HEAL THE BROKEN-HEARTED

A broken heart is much worse than any physical sickness. Many wonderful men of medicine can heal broken bodies. Only Jesus can heal a broken heart. The devil causes men to lie, cheat, steal, murder, commit suicide, and do all manner of evil, but Jesus Christ in the heart gives man the power to overcome the devil. Jesus said His mission in this world was to heal the broken-hearted, and through the Holy Spirit the Christian may heal broken hearts. Jesus promised in Luke 10:16 (NASB), "The one who listens to you, listens to Me." When He said, "I also send you," His next words were, "If you forgive the sins of any, their sins have been forgiven them" (John 20:21-23 NASB). Jesus heals broken hearts today through the lives of obedient Christians. The mission of Jesus in this world was to heal those who were broken-hearted because of sin and the power of Satan. This, then, is the soul-winner's mission.

3.C. PREACH DELIVERANCE TO THE CAPTIVES

This does not mean that Jesus came to open the jails. The expression literally reads, "To herald the captives' release." This is a definition of what it means to preach good news to poor people. The word *captives* here pictures not prisoners in jail but prisoners of war who were dragged away into exile by the conqueror. So the devil holds men as captives with no hope of escape by any means of their own. Jesus was commissioned of the Father to stand forth as a herald and to proclaim for them *aphesis*, "release." This is the regular New Testament term for the remission of sins. It means sending them away forever (compare Luke 1:77). This herald announcement is not meaningless speech but the authoritative effective "release" itself. It transfers these captives of Satan into the light and liberty of the sons of God. Jesus said this was His mission in the world. The mission of the soul winner, then, is to preach deliverance to those moral and spiritual captives of Satan.

3.D. RECOVERING OF SIGHT TO THE BLIND

Of course, Jesus restored sight to physically blind people, but this is not the reference here. Jesus said in Luke 10:23 (NASB), as He spoke to His seventy followers, "Blessed are the eyes which see the things you see." Jesus, when He spoke of recovering of sight to the blind, was speaking of restoring sight to the spiritually blind. These are "blind" people who have been brought to a sense of their blindness (Romans 3:20 KJV) and to whom Jesus alone can give the sight of faith. So, as the mission of Jesus was to restore sight to the spiritually blind, it is also the mission of the soul winner.

3.E. SET AT LIBERTY THEM THAT ARE BRUISED

These poor sinners are crushed and shattered by their sin (*tethrausmenoi*, the perfect participle of *thrauo*, which denotes a condition that still continues). Sin wrecks a human life and makes a person feel wretched by the crushing, shattering consequences of this sin. The alcoholic has redness of eyes and wounds without cause. A mother's heart is bruised by a wayward son. The wife is bruised by a faithless husband. People are always bruised and crushed by sin, and Jesus Christ the Savior frees from wretchedness and restores joy and peace. "To send away in release," *aphesis*, speaks of the release from this broken condition. The mission of Jesus was to set at liberty those who are bruised in heart and soul by sin and Satan. This is the mission of the soul winner.

3.F. PREACH THE ACCEPTABLE YEAR OF THE LORD

What a blessed mission Jesus had, and His is the mission of the soul winner. William Manson well said, "Jesus declares God's will to save His people to be immediate, not in some future age, but now is the captive power of sin to be broken, communion with God to be established, and the will of God to be done."[6] This is what Jesus meant when He said, "Preach the acceptable year of the Lord." A new dispensation started with Jesus; a new era began with Him. It is an era acceptable or pleasing to the Lord, because in it His plan of salvation is being carried out through Jesus. People are acceptable to God through faith in Jesus Christ. The power that God sent to earth in Jesus was the power of His love. So Jesus lived and so He taught, and He imparted this same weapon to His disciples. We are sent to tell every creature that because of love, He may be acceptable to God through faith in Christ. This is the mission of the soul winner.

Our mission is in a world of surging literacy and learning, a world of new life in old religions, and hovering over all of it the threat of holocaust and worldwide destruction. To our task we must bring all that we are, all that we have.

Our mission is all pervading. This means many things but primarily two. First, no place or person exists where we are not concerned; and second, no special, racial, or national limits to our mission can exist.

Oh, does not your heart cry within you! A thousand tribes yet remain unaware of the love of God in Christ! Millions of people have never heard the name of Jesus. Millions are living in total spiritual darkness, having never heard the gospel as we understand it. If we believe that Jesus is coming again and that He may come at any moment, then must we not give ourselves in unhesitating obedience that we may fulfill the mission that He has given us? If we fail Him now in refusing to go forth with Him as He commands us to do, what are we going to say to Him then when we stand in His glorious presence?

Any Christian who will study what God's Word has to say on these things we have discussed must acknowledge: (1) apart from Jesus Christ there is no hope; (2) God has given a clear command to go; and (3) the responsibility is ours as individual Christians. One question remains: will you go? He has commanded it and He will enable you. Do you dare to refuse? Our mission is to share the Lord Jesus Christ with the people in this world. Paul wrote to the Corinthian church in 2 Corinthians 5:18, 20 (NASB), "Now all these things are from God, who reconciled us to Himself through Christ and gave us the ministry of reconciliation. . . . Therefore, we are ambassadors for Christ, as though God were making an appeal through us; we beg you on behalf of Christ, be reconciled to God." Paul wrote in 1 Corinthians 15:34 (NASB), "For some have no knowledge of God. I speak this to your shame."

What a mission is ours, what a challenge is ours—the mission and the challenge of taking the good news to every person in this world, in this acceptable year of the Lord. We must not flinch nor fail in our service to our Savior.

A great contrast exists between the churches of the New Testament and the churches of today. In J. B. Phillips' introduction to *Letters to Young Churches*, he states,

> *The great difference between present-day Christianity and that of which we read in these letters (New Testament Epistles) is that to us it is primarily a performance: to them it was a real experience. We are apt to reduce the Christian religion to a code or, at best, a rule of heart and life. To these men it is quite plainly the invasion of their lives by a new quality of life altogether. They do not hesitate to describe this as Christ living in them.[7]*

The early church was a miracle—a small group of people commissioned by the Lord God of heaven to change the world. We have the same commission.

Peter and Paul were speaking to us when they wrote to believers. Peter said, "But you are a chosen race, a royal priesthood, a holy nation, a people for God's own possession, so that you may proclaim the excellencies of Him who has called you out of darkness into His marvelous light" (1 Peter 2:9 NASB). Paul added, "So that you will prove yourselves to be blameless and innocent, children of God above reproach in the midst of a crooked and perverse generation, among whom you appear as lights in the world" (Philippians 2:15 NASB). Let us look at the warped and diseased world, this wayward world in which we live.

CHAPTER 4

THE SOUL-WINNER'S MILIEU

W. H. Auden described the people of our world as people who are,

Lost in a haunted wood,
Children afraid of the night
Who have never been happy or good.[8]

Men are lost in a haunted wood—haunted by the ghosts of futility, helplessness, insecurity, and fear. Robert Luccock tells of a school boy who wrote in an essay, "I believe so many twins are born into the world today because little children are frightened of entering the world alone."[9] A young mother asked the salesman if the toy he recommended was rather complicated for a small child. He answered, "It's an educational toy, Madam, designed to help the child adjust himself to the world of today. Any way he puts it together is wrong."[10] Never in the history of the world has there been as much unrest as we see today. Half of the world trembles on the border of chaos. The world seethes and boils with hatred, bloodshed, and the lust for power. The world is torn and embittered, sick and suffering, confused and bewildered. Man lives his days in the dominion of darkness rather than in the kingdom of light. He walks in darkness and does not know where he is going.

We may say that we are not to blame for the darkness, the misery, the hunger in our world. Perhaps not altogether. But, do we care? Did Elizabeth Barrett Browning describe you when she wrote,

The human race
To you, means such a child or such a man
You saw one morning waiting in the cold
Beside that gate, perhaps. . . . Why I call you hard
To general suffering. . . .
Does one of you
Stand still from dancing, stop from stringing pearls
And pine and die because of the great sum
Of universal anguish? . . . You cannot count
That you should weep for what you know. A red-haired child,
Sick in a fever, if you touch him once,
Though but so little as with a finger-tip
Will set you weeping—But a million sick?
You could as soon weep for the rule of three
Or compound fractions. Therefore, this same world,
Uncomprehended by you, must remain
Uninfluenced by you. . . .
We get no Christ from you.[11]

Look at the world!

4.A. WE SEE A WORLD IN NEED OF CHRIST

More than two thousand years have gone by since that morning when the angel said to the women who were first at the tomb, "Go quickly and tell." But the story has not yet reached two-thirds of the world's population. These people are still sitting in the shadow of death. No one has told them that Christ has come to conquer sin, death, and hell. Every day there are more pagans and heathens and infidels being born into the world than being converted through saving faith in Christ. More lost people exist today than there were when William Carey went to India in 1792. And we need to remember that the non-Christian world is not geographical.

The world's population is increasing faster than the Bible-believing Christian population. The number of Christians in the world is increasing, but not fast enough. Every person on earth should have a Bible, but all the world's printing presses are not printing nearly enough. Many languages of the world have no Word of God on their tongue. Everyone should have access to a church and a preacher, but there are not enough to go around.

4.B. WE LIVE IN A DAY OF GREAT URGENCY

The millions of the world are astir. The Africans stand questioning, wondering which way to go. The peoples of Asia are on the march. Youth searches for new heroes. This is a day of world choice.

4.B.1. LOOK AT AMERICA

American people are growing up ignorant of the Bible and the God of the Bible. Northwestern University made a survey of religious knowledge of junior high pupils. It found that fifty-two percent did not know in what part of the Bible the life of Jesus is found; sixty-two percent did not know that Jesus had taught the Lord's Prayer; fifty-one percent could not recognize His most familiar parable.[12]

The western part of the United States is big, about the size of India, and there are more than forty million people living in that section of our country. California, Oregon, Washington, Montana, Wyoming, Idaho, Utah, New Mexico, Arizona, Colorado, Nevada, North Dakota, South Dakota, Nebraska, and Kansas are open for the gospel, and only about thirty-five percent of their people are churched.

Though most of the people are unchurched, many religious groups operate in the West. Currently in Los Angeles, many Buddhist temples and Shinto shrines proclaim what they think is the truth. Jehovah's Witnesses are hard at work. Roman and Greek Catholicism bid for the people. The Mormons are very strong, and in recent years they have opened a six-million-dollar temple in Los Angeles on a 224-acre plot of ground. There are all kinds of "isms" in the West, and Aimee McPherson's "Four-Square Gospel" has a grip on many people.[13]

The West has a great need for morality. One thinks particularly of Nevada. Reno is the divorce capital of the world, and it is also a large gambling center. In many of the homes that I visited in Nevada, I found that the husbands and wives had been married several times. The effect on the children is, of course, terrible. "As the home goes, so goes the nation." Las Vegas is the gambling capital of the nation. Scores of gambling halls with all kinds of gambling devices and games of chance and all kinds of lewd entertainment are to be found there. It is almost impossible to imagine the thousands of people who gamble there, and it is pathetic to see small children locked in cars or standing outside the casinos looking in, while their parents shoot dice, play poker, or play slot machines on the inside. A startling fact is that one of every five deaths in Las Vegas is a suicide.

Plainly stated, the West needs Christ. To realize that seventy-two percent of California's people, and almost eighty percent of the people of Washington and

Oregon, make no religious profession, is to realize something of the tremendous need. And to know that many of the others have not heard the true gospel simply underscores the need. Several thousand towns and villages in the West have no evangelical witness.

The great Northeastern section of our nation was once the cradle of the evangelical faith, but now most of the churches are cold and formal, and almost all of the professing Christians who live there are Christians in name only. It has been my privilege to spend six weeks in Pennsylvania in the past two years, and I have seen the great spiritual need there.

The pattern of low-commitment marriage and quick divorce has taken hold in our land. This is a day of divorce and suffering. Broken homes mean broken lives. The Christian faith was once nurtured in the home; it was taught at Mother's knee. Today, most parents are too busy with many things to be concerned with this important thing of religious training in the home. They are depending on the half hour per week in Sunday school to provide the needed religious training of the children, or they ignore the need altogether.

This is a time of great hopes but also of terrible frustrations and disappointments on the part of the American people. Our prosperity is in sharp contrast to the insecurity in this atomic and digital age. An Associated Press release in the New Orleans *States-Item*, November 27, 1962, stated that possibly two million living Americans have tried to commit suicide at least once! About 19,500 suicides are reported annually, but the actual number is probably closer to twenty-five thousand.

4.B.2. LOOK AT EUROPE

Europe was for centuries the lighthouse of the gospel, but now the lighthouse is almost dark. Less than nine percent of the people of Great Britain go to church.

France is almost completely secularized. Spain and Italy are controlled by a hierarchical system which preaches the Virgin Mary and a dead Christ. Most of Western Europe is dominated by some form of state church, either Catholic or Protestant. Eastern Europe still suffers from its time being closed off by the Iron Curtain, and life is difficult for an evangelical Christian.

4.B.3. LOOK AT AFRICA

Asia and Europe are blighted by Communism, South America is in the grip of Romanism, North America is plagued with materialism. Africa stands uncertain and undecided. It is torn between Communism, Islam, Romanism, the prosperity gospel, and evangelical Christianity. Into this delicate balance we must pour every consecrated effort to win Africa for Christ. The message of Christ—redemption, release, peace—is the message for needy Africa.

According to a leading authority on African affairs, out of every ten converts in Africa today, seven become Muslims and three become Christians. During the past thirty years, the Muslim advance has moved nearly one thousand miles farther south. Islam's appeal to Africans lies mainly in its lack of a color bar, its brotherhood, and its simple life which does not have the stigma of being European. I have heard the call of the muezzin to prayer, and my blood has run cold in my veins. And I am reminded of a poem quoted in New Orleans Baptist Theological Seminary Chapel many years ago. Miss May Perry, veteran missionary to Nigeria, quoted the words of an African chief:

Why Didn't You Tell Us Sooner

Why didn't you tell us sooner?
the words come soft and low.
O ye who know the Gospel truths,
Why didn't you let us know?
The Saviour died for all the world,
He died to save from woe,
But we never heard the story—
Why didn't you let us know?
Hear this pathetic cry of ours,
O dwellers in Christian lands!
For Africa stands before you,
With pleading, outstretched hands.
You may not be able to come yourself,
But some in your stead can go:
Will you not send us teachers?
Will you not let us know?
—An African Chief[14]

All across Africa one is impressed by the fact that the people are lost. Idol worship is seen on every hand. One wants to cry with Paul, "The God who made the world and all things in it, since He is Lord of heaven and earth, does not dwell in temples made with hands; nor is He served by human hands, as though He needed anything, since He Himself gives to all people life and breath and all things" (Acts 17:24-25 NASB).

4.B.4. LOOK AT THE MIDDLE EAST

Probably one hundred twenty million people live in the Middle East, and most of them are lost. The Jews of Israel are either without any faith or are following dead rituals. The crescent of Islam hangs over every land in the Middle East, and the muezzin's call to prayer is heard everywhere. Poverty, ignorance, suffering on every hand, and day by day they die in their lost condition.

4.B.5. LOOK AT THE ORIENT

Here live more than one-half of the world's people, and only one in two hundred fifty is an evangelical Christian. China's teeming millions are tragically lost. The Protestant population in China is estimated at seven hundred thousand to one million people. For one hundred years, the doors of China were open, but we failed to take full advantage of the opportunity. Now the doors are closed, and not one evangelical missionary is officially in China today.

Myanmar (formerly Burma) is the oldest American Baptist mission field in the world. Over one hundred fifty years ago, Adoniram Judson began his work there. But we failed to take advantage of the open door we had for so many years. About three percent of the people of Myanmar are Christians today. A 1957 report showed 196,000 Baptists there, the largest Baptist mission field so far as membership in the churches is concerned.

Vietnam is a picture of lostness. Less than one-fifth of one percent of the people are evangelical Christians. These precious people need the gospel. They need Jesus!

The nation of India with one billion people is a land of spiritual darkness. If one preached in eight different villages each day, it would take more than two hundred fifty years to get around to the villages that do not have the gospel!

In Thailand there are more Buddhist temples than there are Christian people. One evangelical Christian exists for every 832 people. In the United States, one evangelical preacher ministers for every six hundred forty people, but in Thailand the ratio is one to more than two hundred thousand people.

Indonesia is a land of promise. Indonesia is a land of need. About 175 million people live there, and about eighty-five percent of them are followers of Islam. Indonesia has one doctor for every fifty-seven thousand people as opposed to one for every eight hundred in the United States. I can never forget the incident related by Dr. Keith Parks of the Baptist Seminary in Semarang on the island of Java. He told of driving home from the seminary with his five-year-old son. As they came down the hill from the campus and reached the main street, they had to stop because thousands of Chinese people were marching along, four abreast.

The son said, "Daddy, where are all those people going?"

Keith answered, "They're going to worship their ancestors."

"What are ancestors, Daddy?"

"Ancestors are dead people."

"Daddy, dead people isn't Jesus."

"I know it, Son."

"Well, Daddy, why don't they worship Jesus?"

Keith tried to explain that they didn't know about Jesus. The child wanted to know why we don't tell them about Jesus. Keith told him there just aren't enough Christians there to tell all the people about Jesus. But a five-year-old boy doesn't stop asking questions, and this boy then drove the knife into his Daddy's heart as he asked, "When are we going to tell them about Jesus?"

And the father had to say, through his tears, "At the rate we're going, we'll never tell them about Jesus."

Hong Kong, with its teeming millions of people, presents a challenge almost unparalleled. About three million people are crowded into a land area less than one-third the size of the state of Rhode Island. Many of these people are poorly fed, are poorly housed, and have come from Red China looking for refuge. And most of them have found no refuge for the soul.

Korea has suffered much in recent years, first from Japanese occupation and then from the Korean War. Her sufferings have helped to make the Korean people very receptive to the gospel. Only about four percent of the people are evangelical Christians. Dr. Wallace Mervin, executive secretary for the Far East of the National Council of Churches Division of Foreign Missions, calls South Korea, "One country in Asia that could become a Christian nation in the foreseeable future."

Japan has about one hundred fifteen million people and only .3 percent of them are evangelical Christians. Doors are wide open in Japan, and now is the time to enter them. If I close my eyes, I can see again the thronging multitudes I saw there in 1957. I see again the thousands of Japanese babies and children, and my heart fills with tears as I realize that their chances of knowing Jesus are slim. I shall never forget the Sunday I left New Orleans for Japan. My baby Charlotte, only two years old then, awakened me that morning by shaking the sides of her baby bed and singing, "Jesus loves me, this I know, for the Bible tells me so." If Japanese children I saw live to be one hundred years old, at the rate we are evangelizing, Japan they will never know Him! They will never be able to sing that song!

At least fifty percent of Australia's people live beyond the influence of the Christian fellowship. The words of Dr. Winston Crawley ring in my ears:

Now is the time for a greatly intensified mission effort in Asia. In an age of revolution and opportunity such as this, "missions as usual" simply will not do.

To understand why "missions as usual" will not do today, it is enough simply to look at Asia: countless multitudes of people, many of them hungry and clothed in rags, most of them without adequate schools and hospitals, nearly all have no knowledge of the love of God and the gospel of Christ, and all filled with new yearnings and hopes and with a determination one way or another to change the world. Then, see beside them our little band of missionaries—about one for every 800,000 people in the lands where we labor. God is blessing them and working miracles through them, but what are so few among so many? Obviously, "missions as usual" will not do. Now, surely, is God's time for Southern Baptists to start a tremendous new forward push in Asia.[15]

Hear this poem by John Oxenham:

I hear a clear voice calling, calling,
Calling out of the night,
O, you who live in the Light of Life,
Bring us the Light!
We are bound in the chains of darkness,
Our eyes have received no sight,
O, you who have never been bond or blind,
Bring us the Light!
You cannot—you shall not forget us,
Out here in the darkest night,
We are drowning men, we are dying men,
Bring, bring us the light! [16]

4.B.6. LOOK AT LATIN AMERICA

Over two hundred million people in Latin America from Mexico to Argentina, and only one in sixty-three is an evangelical Christian. Most of the people are nominally Roman Catholic, but most of the nations of Latin America are open to the gospel. One of the greatest challenges of our day lies in Brazil, a land of about one hundred forty million people. The population is growing at the rate of almost two million per year. Billy Graham said recently, after his South American tour, that opportunity is ours today. "I believe Brazil today is the country widest open to the gospel," he asserted.[17] One of our missionaries told me during my visit to Brazil in 1959 that a Baptist church can be started anywhere in Brazil if there is a preacher and a place for him to preach.

A leading Brazilian Baptist visited the campus of New Orleans Baptist Theological Seminary recently and reported that we have only about eight hundred workers in churches related to vocations in Brazil—213 Southern Baptist missionaries and six hundred national workers.

Many people raise the question: Why go to Latin America? The Roman Catholic Church claims at least ninety percent of the people as members. Aren't these people already Christians? The answer to that was brought vividly to my attention in Santiago, Chile, five years ago. I stood on a hill above the city and looked at a tremendous statue of the Virgin Mary. She stood with the world at her feet, and her foot was placed on the head of a serpent. The guide said to me, "The Bible teaches that the Woman shall crush the head of the serpent." Not so! The Bible teaches that the Seed of the woman shall crush the head of the serpent (Genesis 3:15 KJV). The Virgin Mary cannot save, and a dead Christ will not do! Most of the people of Latin America are lost, but a hunger exists on the part of many for the Word of God.

4.B.7. LOOK AT OTHER WORLD RELIGIONS

A resurgence of the Old World religions is happening now. Islam, a monument to the failure of Christians to evangelize in the seventh and eighth centuries, is on the march again. All over Nigeria I saw Muslim missionaries peddling bicycles to remote villages, carrying the message of the Koran. Somehow we have failed in our attempts to evangelize the Muslims. J. B. Phillips quotes a letter from a missionary to Africa:

> So little has been the impact of Christianity on the Muslims that they do not oppose missionary work among them because they fear no success on the part of the Christians. This is a Muslim stronghold, but the Muslims welcome our going here to bring any help we can. I don't think they fear any conversions.[18]

Hinduism is having a new day in India. Dr. Gaines Dobbins, in a recent address in the New Orleans Baptist Theological Seminary Chapel, said that Hindus said to him during his visit to India, "We have the answer for our world."

Buddhism has become aggressively missionary. Buddhists are now sending missionaries to the United States. They believe that they have an answer. As I travelled through the Orient, I saw many evidences of the resurgence of Buddhism. We believe Jesus is the light of the world. But in one of the main streets of Colombo (Ceylon), among the decorations celebrating the twenty-five hundredth anniversary of Buddhism, a great statue of the Buddha was erected. By an ingenious arrangement of electric lights, rays from Buddha fell upon the surface of a great globe of the world, slowly rotating on its axis a few feet away. Across the whole structure stood out the superscription, *The Light of the World.*

4.B.8. LOOK AT COMMUNISM/MARXISM

Communism is on the march. Is Communism perhaps God's judgment on the church? Communism has a real appeal for many people. It promises a classless society in which men would be free from economic and political slavery. It claims to have a message for the "forgotten man." And Communism has a missionary zeal unmatched by modern enterprise.

A young communist in Italy said, "I did not join the party for ideological reasons. I had not then read a line of Marx. I did not adhere to a philosophy when I joined the Party. I joined the struggle and I joined men."

When one becomes a communist, he knows he has a message which will attract many people. He looks on Communism somewhat as the early Christians looked on the gospel—here is something to be shared. For only as he draws others into the communist movement will there be a speeding up of the processes of history which he believes are on the side of Communism. It takes many people to create a revolution which will destroy the church and capitalism and thus turn the whole world over to the proletariat. A communist writer said,

> We communists do not play with words. We are realists. Seeing we are determined to achieve our object; we know how to obtain the means. Of our salaries and wages we keep only that which is strictly   necessary and we give up the rest for propaganda purposes. To this propaganda we concentrate all our   free time and part of our holidays. You only give a little time and money to the spread of the gospel. How can anyone believe in the supreme value of the gospel if you do not practice it, if you do not spread it, and if you sacrifice neither time nor money for it? Believe me, it is we who will win, for we believe in our Communist message and we are ready to sacrifice anything, everything, even our life in order that social justice shall triumph. But you people are afraid to soil your hands.[19]

It is significant that the Communist Manifesto was issued in 1848, about the same time that treaties were signed which opened China's interior to missionaries. In the following century, Christians often failed to enter open doors, but the communists became increasingly active.

The communists believe something. Their challenge cannot be met by doubts, by simple social service, or by an appeal to goodness. Communism permits no neutrality. It demands conformity—it claims the whole of life.

In pre-World War II China, a Chinese girl was being put to death for being a communist. Her relatives surrounded her; their faces streaked with tears. Hers was the only calm face. "You are weeping for me," she said, "you should weep for yourselves. I am dying for a cause . . . you will go on living—for what?"

It is very easy to underrate the adversaries of the Christian faith. The denial in Catholic Spain of religious liberty has seriously crippled the evangelical cause and denied too many people the privilege of hearing the glorious gospel. The heel of Communism on the neck of the churches of Eastern Europe greatly limited their witness. Outside forces can and do hurt the work of the churches. Let us remember history. Twice in China and once in North Africa the Christian witness has been almost completely stamped out. The non-Christian population of our world is growing much faster than the Christian population. Mankind finds it easier to produce babies than Christians to produce Christians. This is a wayward world in which we live.

Paul said in 2 Corinthians 4:3-4 (NASB), "And even if our gospel is veiled to those who are perishing, in whose case the god of this world has blinded the minds of the unbelieving so that they might not see the light of the gospel of the glory of Christ, who is the image of God."

4.C. MEN ARE LOST WITHOUT CHRIST

The gospel is set against the background of man's sin. We do not need to create an issue—the issue is already here. It is sin and salvation. The world never tells the sinner that he is a sinner under the wrath of God, but God's Word does! "He who believes in Him is not judged; he who does not believe has been judged already, because he has not believed in the name of the only begotten Son of God. . . . He who believes in the Son has eternal life; but he who does not obey the Son will not see life, but the wrath of God abides on him" (John 3:18, 36 NASB).

We must realize that men are dead in trespasses and sins, that there is no good thing in any man, or we will not do much in evangelism. Men are lost without Christ. They may be attractive, educated, and cultured, but without Christ they are lost. All are lost without Christ. Paul knew this—Acts 20:31 (NASB) says that "I did not cease to admonish each one with tears."

Lost means having missed the way, and Jesus said, "I am the way, and the truth, and the life; no one comes to the Father but through Me" (John 14:6 NASB). All are lost who do not know the way home. Yet even among evangelical

Christians, there are those who no longer believe that people who have not trusted in Christ for salvation are truly spiritually lost. But did not Paul say, "And even if our gospel is veiled, it is veiled to those who are perishing" (2 Corinthians 4:3 NASB)? John said, "We know that we are of God, and that the whole world lies in the power of the evil one" (1 John 5:19 NASB).

Was there ever a time when so little sense of the sinfulness of sin existed, so little holiness among professing Christians? Eugene Harrison said in 1850 that it took five Christians in America to lead one person to Christ in a year; in 1900 it took fourteen; in 1919 it took twenty-one; in 1954 it took thirty-three Christians to lead one person to Christ in a year.[20] Jack Stanton of the Division of Evangelism, Southern Baptist Convention, says it now takes one hundred.

Many people ask, *Are the heathen really lost if they have never heard of the gospel?* This is not the real question. The real question is, *Are we really saved if we don't give them the gospel?* For our world, it is Christ or nothing! Perhaps we may sum up these remarks about a wayward world like this: A preacher preached on missions one day, then led in the observance of the Lord's Supper. Glancing at the cup in hand, he suddenly envisioned the faces of millions of pagans, dying without God. Later he wrote,

> *Suddenly, before my inward, opened vision,*
> *Millions of faces crowded up to view,*
> *Sad eyes that said, "For us there is no provision;*
> *Give us your savior, too.*
> *Give us your cup of consolation—*
> *See, to our outstretched hands 'tis never passed.*
> *Yet ours is the desire of every nation—and*
> *Oh, God, we die so fast.*[21]

For you see, at every breath we draw, four souls perish, never having heard of Christ. This is the soul-winner's milieu.

CHAPTER 5

THE SOUL-WINNER'S MOTIVATION

What motivates us to go as witnesses? It seems to me it is a four-fold motivation.[22] Now that we understand the great need around us, we must be moved to do something about it, something that will have eternal consequences.

5.A. THE CALL FROM ABOVE IS ENOUGH

Christ in heaven has commanded that we go. This is the call from above that cannot be ignored by the New Testament believer. Each of the four Gospels make the imperative commands of Christ clear to every believer.

5.A.1. MATTHEW 28:18-20 (NASB)

And Jesus came up and spoke to them, saying, "All authority has been given to Me in heaven and on earth. Go therefore and make disciples of all the nations, baptizing them in the name of the Father and the Son and the Holy Spirit, teaching them to observe all that I commanded you; and lo, I am with you always, even to the end of the age."

Go and tell!

5.A.2. MARK 16:15 (NASB)

And He said to them, "Go into all the world and preach the gospel to all creation."

Go and tell!

5.A.3. LUKE 24:46-48 (NASB)

And He said to them, "Thus it is written, that the Christ would suffer and rise from the dead the third day, and that repentance for forgiveness of sins would be proclaimed in His name to all the nations, beginning from Jerusalem. You are witnesses of these things."

Go and tell!

5.A.4. JOHN 20:21 (NASB)

So Jesus said to them again, "Peace be with you; as the Father has sent Me, I also send you."

Go and tell!

5.A.5. ACTS 1:8 (NASB)

"But you will receive power when the Holy Spirit has come upon you; and you shall be My witnesses both in Jerusalem, and in all Judea and Samaria, and even to the remotest part of the earth."

The very fact that our Lord and Master has commanded us to be witnesses for Him is enough to send us out.

Go and tell!

5.B. THE CALL FROM BENEATH

The cry of those who have lived and died without Christ is enough to send us out. Jesus related the experience of a man who at death was irrevocably separated from God. This man cried to Abraham, "Then I beg you, father, that you send him to my father's house—for I have five brothers—in order that he may warn them, so that they will not also come to this place of torment" (see Luke 16:19-31 NASB). The cry of those who have lived and died without the Savior is enough to send us out.

The doctrine of hell is seldom preached from today's pulpits. Yet most of the information about hell in the New Testament comes from the Lord Jesus Himself. We must remember that the God of love is also the God of truth.

5.C. THE CALL FROM WITHOUT

The heart cry of the lost all around us is sufficient motive for going. Many people in our world are longing for salvation in Jesus, some without even knowing what they are longing for. Some time ago, I went with a pastor to talk with a thirty-four-year-old man about Christ. We asked if we could talk with him about salvation. He began to weep and said, "I wish you would. I grew up in a Baptist home and went to Sunday school and church all my life. But no one ever told me how to be saved, and before I knew it, I was a man, and unsaved. I was ashamed to tell anyone I didn't know how to be saved and have hoped for years that someone would come and tell me."

Dear Old "Mother" Lee in Henderson, Tennessee, eighty-one years old, walked one mile to 7 a.m. services and gave her testimony. She was thirty-three years old when saved. She wanted to be saved before, but she had no opportunity to go to church as a young person and no one told her how to be saved. A fifty-five-year-old man in Mississippi was saved when the Bible message was presented to him. His wife said they had been married for thirty-four years, and no one had ever before told him from the Bible that he needed to be saved. She indicted herself, her pastor, her church!

5.D. THE CALL FROM WITHIN

We go because we have received the good news, and Jesus is our Savior. The normal person who learns something good wants to share it with others. If we are saved, our hearts are filled with something which we must share.

I don't believe anybody in the world who has had a personal experience with Jesus can fail to tell other people about Him. A compulsion is present, a drive goes on, an urgency stays in our souls if we really know the Lord. If we have the joy of salvation, if we have the joy of forgiveness of sins, then we know that other people need this, we know that they want it, and the desire in our hearts is that they should have it. Dr. Perry Webb, Sr., said, "If you have it, you'll tell it. Do you have it?" If you have it, you'll tell it. Do you have it? I just don't believe that a person can really be saved and not want other people to be saved.

The greatest compulsion is not the command of our Lord, as great as that is. The greatest compulsion is not the fact that we know people have died and have gone to hell, as great as that compulsion is. The greatest compulsion to go as witnesses for Christ is not the fact that people are lost around us and want to be saved, as great as that compulsion is. The greatest compulsion for the soul winner, the greatest motivating factor, is the fact that he knows Jesus. He has Jesus in his heart, and this sends him out. All that I've said could actually be reduced to two things: glorifying God and showing the love of God.

5.D.1. WE ARE CALLED TO GLORIFY GOD

We are motivated to be soul winners in order that God may be glorified. The person who knows Jesus desires that God be glorified. Jesus prayed before He was crucified, "I glorified You on the earth, having accomplished the work which You have given Me to do" (John 17:4 NASB). Then He spoke to His disciples, "Let your light shine before men in such a way that they may see your good works, and glorify your Father who is in heaven" (Matthew 5:16 NASB). Jesus said again in John 15:8 (NASB), "My Father is glorified by this, that you bear much fruit, and so prove to be My disciples." As Paul stood and looked at the city of Athens, his heart was broken. He saw these people who knew about God and who in times past had known more about God, and he saw that they had given themselves over completely to idolatry. He wrote in Romans 1:21, 23 (NASB), "For even though they knew God, they did not honor Him as God or give thanks, but they became futile in their speculations, and their foolish heart was darkened. . . . and exchanged the glory of the incorruptible God for an image in the form of corruptible man and of birds and four-footed animals and crawling creatures." And in verse 25, "For they exchanged the truth of God for a lie, and worshipped and served the creature rather than the Creator, who is blessed forever. Amen." A great motivating factor is the desire to glorify God. The person who knows the Lord wants to glorify Him.

5.D.2. WE ARE CALLED TO SHOW THE LOVE OF GOD

The second summary statement is that love motivates. Love compels. When Jesus was asked what is the first and greatest commandment, He didn't say, "Keep the Sabbath day." He didn't say, "Don't covet." He didn't say, "Don't commit adultery." He said, "You shall love the LORD your God with all your heart and with all your soul and with all your might" (Deuteronomy 6:5 NASB). With everything that you are and everything that you have, you are to love God. And so, the great motivating factor is love. Jesus said in John 14:23 (NASB), "If anyone loves Me, he will keep My word; and My Father will love him, and We will come to him and make Our abode with him." He said again in John 15:9, 10 (KJV), "Just as the Father has loved Me, I have also loved you; abide in My love." If you keep My commandments, you will abide in My love; just as I have kept My Father's commandments and abide in His love." Obedience is always the evidence of true love for God. This is the measuring stick for the Christian. Is that not what Jesus said?

By the way, when one is out witnessing and a man begins to hedge on following through with what he says is a commitment to Christ, those verses from John's Gospel are good verses to read to him. "Do you love Jesus? If you love Jesus, you'll be obedient to Him." Now, Jesus said it very plainly. He didn't hesitate at all. We probably have sugar-coated it a little bit, but Jesus didn't do it. He said, "If anyone loves Me, he will keep My word; and My Father will love him, and We will come to him and make Our abode with him" (John 14:23 KJV). That is plain, isn't it? In fact, it is so plain that most of us are afraid to use it, but it is a good thing to say to people. Jesus said if you love Him, you'll do what He says. If you don't love Him, you'll not do what He says. Do you really love Jesus?

Three years ago, I was in one of our pioneer mission churches in Pennsylvania and went out to talk to a young couple about moving their membership into the church. They were from Tennessee, both of them Southern Baptists. They had been living there at that time for about six months, and they had never moved their membership. They could have thrown a rock and hit the little Southern Baptist church. We went into their trailer home and started talking with them, and they told us that they were Southern Baptists. One of them belonged to one church, and the other belonged to another church. They had been married just a brief time, a year and a half or so, but had never put their membership in the same church.

When we talked to them about moving their membership, they said, "We haven't decided what church we are going to join." That happened to be the only Southern Baptist church within twenty miles, so I asked them how far they planned to drive to church. "Not far," they said.

I said, "Then you don't have any decision to make; the church is right here. You're Southern Baptists, and this is a Southern Baptist church—the decision is already made. It's even the closest church of any denomination."

They hesitated again, and said, "Well, we don't know how long we are going to be here."

And finally, the boy said, "I'll be here for twenty more months, and then I'm going back to Tennessee." Twenty months! He said, "There is no use moving my membership. I'll just be here twenty months."

I said, "Sir, that is almost two years, and if the Lord delays His coming, don't you want to serve Him for these two years?"

He began to hesitate again. Finally, he was pressed into a corner and became belligerent. I asked him if I could ask him just one question and then leave. He said yes, and I reminded him of the things he had said—that he had

had a real experience with the Lord, he was a Southern Baptist, and he was baptized into the fellowship of a Baptist church down in Tennessee. And I went through all the things we had talked about.

Then I said, "This is the question: do you really love Jesus?"

He got red in the face, thought for a minute or two, and said, "Yes, Sir, I really do."

I opened my New Testament and read to him from the fourteenth chapter of John what Jesus said. I said, "I'm not going to tell you what you ought to do, but I'm going to ask you as a child of God who loves the Lord Jesus, would you pray about this thing and ask Him what He wants you to do? He said if you love Him, you'll be obedient."

He and his wife came and moved their membership that night. I went back about a year later, and they were very active in that church, serving the Lord.

Obedience is the real measure of discipleship. If we love Jesus, we'll be obedient. Love is the motivating factor, and it motivates us to obedience to the Lord.

Paul wrote to the Corinthians and said (1 Corinthians 15:4 Allison translation), "For the love of Christ controls us, having concluded this, that one died for all, therefore all died." It is the love of Christ that really motivates us.

When they began building the campus of New Orleans Baptist Theological Seminary, my wife and I lived on Dement Street in one of the apartment buildings. I went to school on the "old campus" but lived on the "new campus." They were building some of the other apartment buildings on Dement Street, and our little girl, who was not quite two years old at the time, disappeared one afternoon. We looked for her all over the campus. We couldn't find her anywhere and really became alarmed. Those buildings were half completed, with rough stairs up to the second floor. We had all kinds of visions about what could have happened to her, as you can imagine. We looked, we called, and we went everywhere, but we couldn't find her. Finally, after about an hour of searching, we found her in an apartment. She had just wandered up to someone's apartment and knocked on the door. When they came to the door, she went right in and sat down and started playing—unconcerned! But we were concerned. What drove us to look for her? What drove us to try to find the child who was lost? It was love! We loved her, and we wanted to find her. Love always drives us out to seek those who are lost. This is the great motivating factor—if we love people, we'll love their souls. If we love their souls, we will want to see them saved. So the great motivation is our love for the Lord Jesus. If we love Him, we will be obedient.

An interesting account has been passed down of the advance of the Muslim empire across the Middle East and then on across North Africa. About 277 years after the death of Mohammed, one of the Muslim preachers took upon himself a number of very imposing titles. He began to call himself the Guide, the Director, the Demonstration, the Representative of Mohammed, John the Baptist, Gabriel, the Herald of Messiah, the Word, the Holy Ghost, and a number of other names. He drew around him a group of followers who were very fanatical in their love for him, and, therefore, in their obedience to him. He began to move against the enemies of Islam. His followers went out all over the Middle East and across North Africa, preaching and winning disciples to this man. The people there actually were ready for rebellion. But the secret of the power of this man was the blind obedience of his followers because of their love for him. He went to a strategic city to try to take the city, sent an emissary in, and asked for one of the leaders to come out and talk with him.

The leader came to talk with him at the gates of the capital. The man who had come to seize the city, the great Arabian preacher, said to the leader of the forces within the city, "I have come to take this city. Your master has 30,000 troops at his disposal here, and I have just a handful of men. But in all the 30,000 that he has, he doesn't have three such as I have." He called three of his men. He said to one of them, "I want you to plunge a dagger into your chest." He said to another one, "I want you to jump into the Tigris River." He told the third he wanted him to throw himself off a precipice. All three of these men did as he asked with unquestioning obedience. They didn't say a word; they simply did what he told them to do. The preacher said to the leader of the forces within the city, "You go tell your master what you have seen, and before night falls, your master is going to be chained with my dogs." And he was![23] The forces in the city were terribly frightened. To say to a man, "Plunge a dagger in your chest," and he does it; to another "jump into the Tigris River and drown," and he does it; to another, "jump off a precipice," and he does it—this is frightening! Unquestioning obedience they showed because of their love for their master. And a whole city fell, just because these three men were obedient.

No way of predicting the future exists in this world, and we have no way to know what would happen to the strongholds of Satan, if God's people were unquestioningly obedient to the Lord. Nothing really seems as simple as obeying the Lord, does it? We have prayer and we have the Bible and we can know what the Lord wants us to do. It seems that it ought to be the simplest thing in the world just to be obedient to the Lord. What do you think could happen in our world if the sixteen million Southern Baptists really became obedient to the Lord—if it were unquestioning obedience? It wouldn't take sixteen million.

What would happen if just those who read this book really became obedient to the Lord?

William Temple, the late Archbishop of Canterbury, in the book *Basic Christianity*, said, "Is it true that God has taken action for the salvation of His people? And is it true that the God who has so taken action—is He of whom the revelation is set before us through the pages of the Bible—the Lord God of Israel? The first element in the divine constraint of Christian missions is the sheer truth of the Gospel."[24]

Temple went on to add, "We have the responsibility of making up our minds whether or not we accept it as the truth. But if we do accept it as the truth, we have no longer any real option in the matter of being or failing to be missionaries. If it is the truth, it lays upon us missionary obligations by the very consideration that it's true."[25] He said if the Bible is the Word of God, if it is really true, then we don't have anything else to do except to be obedient to the Lord and to be witnesses for Him—missionaries for Him. The one thing we have to decide: Is the Word of God really true? If you believe the Bible, then you are to be a witness wherever you are. Is the Bible the Word of God? Can we take it and believe it and know that it is true? If this Word is true, then we have no argument at all; if we accept this as true, then we are to be witnesses, we are to be evangelists.

Temple also said in the same book,

> We have gotten into the habit of thinking of religion as a kind of drug for the curing of the world's diseases. So, we ask whether the Gospel suits the African or the Arabian, the Indian, etc. But if the Gospel is true, then the question is not whether it suits us, but whether we suit it, and whether the African suits it, etc. And if we or they don't suit it and if it is the truth, we had better alter ourselves until we do, or rather submit ourselves to the Gospel to alter us. If a thing is true at all, it is true everywhere and always. The Gospel is true for all, if it is true at all.[26]

This is the whole thing in a nutshell. If the gospel is really true, it is true for every person everywhere. And it is not a question of whether the gospel suits us, it is whether we suit the gospel. Obedience—this is what he is saying—obedience. If it is true, we are to be obedient.

Love brings obedience. I say again, love is the great motivation that sends us out to be soul winners. Someone has said, "Love cannot let a sinner alone." The sinner wants to be let alone in his sin—he doesn't want to be disturbed. A man who really is wrapped up in sin is a painful thing. He just doesn't want to be bothered about it. Wasn't the cry of the demons in Christ's day, "Let us alone!"? It is still the cry: "Let us alone!" It is hard to get sinners to go to church services, isn't it? Or is it that way in your community? Do they just flock out to the church to hear the pastor preach? How many times does the pastor preach, when so far as you know there is not a lost person there in the church? Lost sinners don't come often to church. They stay away from the gospel. Most of the lost sinners will choose to stop attending church. They will come a time or two because someone keeps after them. But love can't leave the sinner in his sins any more than light can let darkness alone. One turns on the light and it has to shine out the darkness. And if we love Jesus and love lost people, we can't leave lost people alone.

I went recently and talked with a man I had intended to leave alone. He had told me about his "experience" and what he was going to do about it. But, he had lied every time I'd talked with him since he said he made a commitment to Christ. I finally said, "I'm going to leave him alone—I'm not going back to hear him lie again." But I went back once more, and he lied again. He had suffered a serious heart attack and would have died had he not been taken to the hospital immediately.

As he was recovering, he said, "When I get up from here and am able to go to church, I'll make a public confession of faith." When he was able, he went to Sunday school, but he didn't even stay for the worship service. *Nevertheless, I must go back again.*

When one loves people and loves Jesus, he can't leave the lost ones alone. The real constraint is the heart-hunger of God. God so loved the world that He gave His Son. God commended His love toward us, in that while we were yet sinners, Christ died for us. And it is the heart-hunger of God that is the real constraint—the real compelling motive that sends us out to be witnesses. We claim to rejoice in His love, but we can't really rejoice in it, when that love hungers to reach other people who have never yet even heard of Him. We cannot do a lot of rejoicing in God's love until we are faithful as witnesses to Him. Love drives us out.

Peter said, "But you are a chosen race, a royal priesthood, a holy nation, a people for God's own possession, so that you may proclaim the excellencies of Him who has called you out of darkness into His marvelous light" (1 Peter 2:9 NASB). This idea can be that you are a "purchased people." In order that we might show forth the praises of Him who has called us out of darkness into His marvelous light.

Preachers should preach on soul winning. God promised to go before us (Isaiah 45:2). He promises to go behind us (Isaiah 58:8). He promises to go beneath us (Deuteronomy 33:27). Underneath are the everlasting arms. He promises to go with us (Matthew 28:20). He promises to go within us (John

14:17). He promises to go upon us (Acts 1:8), "The Holy Spirit shall come upon you." He promises to go all around us (Matthew 3:11).

We're talking about motivation—the thing that sends us out. Have you ever heard somebody say, "Well, I believe that if a fellow really lives it, he won't have to say anything about it"? Have you been guilty sometime of saying that yourself? If a man or woman ever again says that to you, ask for Scripture to back it up. You can give him plenty of Scripture which tells us to go and speak, to go and tell. In Romans 10:17 (NASB), the Scripture states, "So faith comes from hearing, and hearing by the word of Christ." Faith does not come by example. Of course, one must live for the Lord Jesus, or His testimony doesn't count for much. But have you seen, and I have seen, the results of preaching when a preacher was not right with the Lord, and you knew he was not right with the Lord; yet the Lord's Word bore fruit? It is God's Word which counts—it is not the person who preaches. It is the Word preached. Paul said to the Corinthians, "For since in the wisdom of God the world through its wisdom did not come to know God, God was well-pleased through the foolishness of the message preached to save those who believe" (1 Corinthians 1:21 NASB). This verse could be understood as, "It pleased God by the foolishness of the thing preached to save them that believe" (Allison translation). It is the gospel—the gospel of Jesus Christ—that is the power of God unto salvation to everyone who believes. Faith comes by hearing and hearing by the Word of God.

Of course, any person who knows Jesus ought to want to live for Him and live like Him. And if a person does know Jesus, he does desire to live like Him. But there is not a person in this world who would dare stand up and say, "I am just like Jesus." If we have to wait until we are just like Him, we will never witness to anybody. Isn't it wonderful that it doesn't depend on our goodness and our perfection? Thank God we don't have to be perfect to be witnesses. And thank God it is not by my life that people are saved—it is through the gospel of Jesus, the good news that Jesus died for our sins, that He was buried, and that He rose again the third day for our justification. Many people are confused about this and we need to tell them what God said. Preach to them that faith comes by hearing and hearing by the Word of God.

Some Christians think that the giving of money meets all of God's requirements for Christian living. They give their money, and they feel that this takes care of all their obligations. Every child of God should give his money—it should start with the tithe, but it ought not to end there. There should be love gifts above the tithe, and we ought to give all that we can give, but if one gives seventy-five percent of his income every week to the Lord's work, it still would not relieve him of the responsibility of being a personal witness for Jesus.

Some people think that prayer meets all God's demands. We are to pray, but prayer is not enough. The same Lord who told us to pray and taught us to pray commanded that we be witnesses for Him. A lady said to me not long ago that she believed she was called to the ministry of intercessory prayer. This is a tremendous ministry, the ministry of intercessory prayer, but there is a danger there. The danger is that one will get so involved interceding for others that he will never go out to bear witness himself. Now, no matter how one prays for others, and no matter what a burden for prayer he has, no matter how sincere he may be, no matter how much power he may have in prayer, he still has the direct responsibility to be a witness.

Organization does not take the place of giving forth the Word of God. We are organized to the nth degree, and I am for organization. One will never get very far if he has no organization. But organization in a church or an individual life does not take the place of witnessing. Dr. R. G. Lee, longtime pastor of Bellevue Baptist Church in Memphis, Tennessee, said one time that if an automobile had as many useless parts as some churches, it wouldn't even run down a hill. That is the truth. Some of our folks attend the meeting of every organization they belong to, and even visit others, but never one time have they witnessed to anybody with the Word of God. Nothing is wrong with organization—but don't try to throw the baby out with the bathwater! Keep the organization but use the organization for the things for which it is intended. Every organization in your church ought to be geared to reaching people for Jesus and then for teaching them to observe the things that He has commanded so they in turn can reach others for Jesus. If the organizations in your church are not doing this, then they have no business existing in your church. Every organization in the church ought to have as its primary purpose the reaching of people for Christ and the training of people to reach others for Christ. But organization itself does not take the place of the proclamation of the gospel.

By this I do not mean just the public proclamation of the gospel. Many people will stand in the pulpit and preach to a hundred people but would not go down the street to talk with one person about the Lord. But it takes both kinds of witnesses. A little secret here is that the folks in your church will never do it if the pastor does not do it. One can get them all fired up and get them out witnessing. Then let that church call a pastor who doesn't witness, and they will quit. The reason you don't have a soul-winning church is because the pastor is not a soul winner; or conversely, the reason you have a soul-winning church is because the pastor is a soul winner.

In the twelfth chapter of Revelation, verse 11, John speaks of those who overcame. John tells us why they overcame. Three reasons are stated: (1) The blood of the lamb, referring to the fact that they had been saved. That is the first thing. (2) The word of their testimony, referring to the fact that they went out and told people about Jesus. And (3) they held not their lives dear unto themselves. They went out and told people even if it meant they were pulled apart, had their heads cut off, were crucified, crucified upside down, etc. Whatever the cost, they went out and told people the good news of Jesus. That is the reason they overcame. They were saved, they were witnesses, and they witnessed no matter what it cost them. This is the overcoming life. "They held not their lives dear unto themselves." Ask yourself, *Am I saved, am I witnessing, will I witness whatever the cost?*

I must tell you an experience of a Christian in Spain, because it so perfectly illustrates what happens to a person who is really in love with Jesus. An old man, seventy-two years old, was arrested for handing out tracts in the streets. In Spain, one cannot hand out religious tracts—it is against the law. He was handing out some gospel tracts and was arrested and carried before the judge. The judge said, "You are charged with handing out religious literature on the streets."

The old man said, "That is right, your Honor, let me show you what I was handing out." He gave a tract to the judge. But the judge gave him thirty days in jail for his trouble. The old man went to jail, and before long, he led four of the prisoners to Christ and had the policemen who were guards on the brink of conversion. They were under conviction.

The authorities said to him, "You can't do that here."

He said, "Oh, yes, you can't do anything to me—I am already in jail."

And then they said to him, "We have commuted your sentence; you don't have to serve the rest of it."

But the man said, "No, sir, you can't do that to me. You sentenced me to thirty days in jail, and I insist on serving the full thirty days. This is the best opportunity I have ever had in my life to witness for Jesus."

Think about that for a moment. He was seventy-two years old, and he wasn't a preacher, either. He was a layman. He said, "I want to serve all of my time because this is the best opportunity I have ever had in my life to witness for Jesus." Let me ask you something: Would you be willing to go to jail just to be able to tell people about the Savior? Most of us are not willing to go across the street to witness. It is something to think about.

One of the most gripping things I've ever read is J. B. Priestley's novel, *Daylight on Saturday*, related and applied by Halford Luccock:

> The novel portrays life in an armament factory in England during World War II, with all the human relationships and problems involved. There is a bitter conflict among the workers, and a superintendent and a workman are talking it over. The superintendent says with a sigh of despair: "We can't even get together to save ourselves from

these devils (the Nazis) without quarrelling among ourselves every five minutes. We're doing a useful job here—an urgent job—as you know—and yet look at us. So I say again—What's the matter with us all?"

"My feeling is," said Sammy, slowly, struggling with his thought, "my   feeling is, Mr. Cheviot, that people 'aven't much to get 'old of. They feel a bit empty inside. They don't know where they're goin' or what it's all about. An' nobody and nothin' tell 'em. Wireless doesn't tell 'em. The films don't tell 'em. The pint or the gin-an'-what's-it they 'ave at the local doesn't tell 'em. The papers don't tell 'em. They're just goin' round in a circle, you might say. You listen to 'em, Mr. Cheviot. They're always sayin' 'So what?' An' it frightens me—that 'So what?'

"But I fancy most o' them don't know neither. If they did an' were certain, th'd come runnin' wi' the good news. An' people listen all right if a proper message comes through.

Will you let those words sink into your mind—"…if they did (know) and were certain, they'd come runnin' wi' the good news." They are truly the words of   God to His Church today. Could any words more clearly express the needed action, for the Church and Christian people today, to "come runnin'" with the Good News to a world that desperately needs it for its salvation?

Here are the three questions: (1) Do you know any good news for the world? (2) Are you sure of it? (3) Will you come runnin' with it?[27]

CHAPTER 6

THE SOUL-WINNER'S MUSTS

We need to consider the qualifications for soul winning. I have been a preacher too long, maybe, but I am always looking for alliteration in order to help me to remember things. Perhaps it will help you too. Let us discuss eight "Ps" in connection with the soul-winner's qualifications.

6.A. THE FIRST MUST: PERSONAL SALVATION

If a man is going to be a soul winner, he first of all must be saved, and he must know that he is saved. No man will ever be an effective soul winner who has doubts about his own salvation. If you doubt whether you are saved, you are not going out to try to help someone else be saved. So personal salvation is essential.

When I was a student in seminary, Dr. A. S. Gillespie was our professor of missions. He left the mission field in China because the communists had driven him out. The first day I went in his missions class, he looked us over rather carefully and said, "Men, are you saved?" I thought that was an awfully strange question to come from a seminary professor to a group of preachers. "Men, are you saved?" And he said, "Don't look at me like that; some men in the seminary are not saved, and there are men out in the pastorate who are not saved. There are music directors who are not saved, and educational men who are not saved, and pastor's wives who are not saved." He said again, "Don't look at me like that! I am asking you an important basic question: are you saved?"

During those days, a man in school with us finished with a master's degree in sacred music and went out to be the minister of music in a church. He was saved during a revival meeting in which he was leading the singing. He went through two years in the seminary. He had been to a Baptist college for four years. He was a preacher's son but was saved after his college and seminary work, after he had been working in a church as minister of music!

This is basic: *Are you saved?* Have you had a real saving experience with Jesus? It is important that you know that you have had a genuine experience with Jesus Christ. I believe with all my heart that a person who is saved knows that he is saved or at least may know that he is saved. First John 5:10-13 (NASB) states,

> *The one who believes in the Son of God has the testimony in himself; the one who does not believe God has made Him a liar, because he has not believed in the testimony that God has given concerning His Son. And the testimony is this, that God has given us eternal life, and this life is in His Son. He who has the Son has the life; he who does not have the Son of God does not have the life. These things I have written to you who believe in the name of the Son of God, so that you may know that you have eternal life.*

John said that he had written to those that believe so that they might know— not guess, not hope, not think, but that you may know that you have eternal life. Somebody may say, "Yes, but look, he said 'and that you may believe on the name of the Son of God.'" This is not contradictory. It means "that your faith then may grow stronger in the Lord Jesus Christ." The father of the mute boy said, "I do believe; help my unbelief" (Mark 9:24 NASB). "Lord, I trust you, I have faith in you: but give me more faith, I am so short of faith." This is what John is saying. If one has been saved, he knows that he is saved, and his faith then will be strengthened day by day.

Must a person be able to go back to a definite time when he is saved? I believe personally that any person who is saved can go back to the experience when he was saved—not necessarily the date, the hour, the minute, but back to a definite experience with Christ. If I had to give you today the date of my salvation, I could not do it. I was saved in August of 1935, on a hot August night during a revival meeting. I do not know the date. The church did not record it, and nobody told me to write it down, so I do not know the date. But I know the experience. That was nearly fifty years ago, and the experience is as vivid as if it happened yesterday. I remember the experience of trusting Christ.

There must be a time when a person makes a commitment. This is basic. We must tell them they need a definite, personal commitment of heart and life for Jesus Christ.

You may say to me, *Brother Allison, are you married?* Well, I certainly am married. *How do you know that you are married?* I live with Voncille. *No, that will not do—there are many couples who live together who are not married.* Well, she has borne three children to me. *No, sad to say, many women bear children to others when they are not married.* Oh, we share an income. *No, people share incomes who are not married.* We share a house and share a car, etc. How do I know that I am married? Because on June 27, 1946, I stood with that girl before a preacher and a church full of folks. The preacher said to me, "Gray, will you take this woman to be your lawful wife, to have and to hold from this day forward, etc., and forsaking all others, cleave only and always to her as long as you both shall live?" And I said out loud to her and to the whole world, "I will." He asked her those questions and she said, "I will." He then said, "I pronounce you man and wife." We were married because we made a commitment of life to each other. I loved her for four years before I married her, but I was married to her when I made a commitment of my life to her and she committed her life to me. It was a double commitment, because Jesus said if a person commits his life to Him, then He will commit real life to that person (the one evangelizing). There must be a definite, conscious experience of turning away from sin and committing of heart and life to Jesus Christ. One can go back to a definite experience of commitment if he has made that commitment.

Do you think I could ever forget when I got married? That is a life-changing experience! I had a thousand, cold cash dollars in the bank. (I have never had any money in the bank since then!) I was young, single, and carefree. From being a carefree bachelor with no responsibility, suddenly I had a woman for whom I was responsible, and the first thing you know, children for whom I was responsible. It was a life-changing experience. Do you think I could ever forget an experience that changed my life as radically as marriage did?

Jesus described the experience of being saved as such a radical experience that He compared it with birth, and He said it is a new birth. It is a completely different life; it is a complete change of life. Do you think I can ever forget making a commitment of my life to a Person when it changed everything in my life—the aim, the direction, the purpose, the scope of my life? How could one forget that kind of commitment? I believe with all my heart that a person who is saved can go back to a definite commitment of life to Jesus Christ. If one can't go back to a definite commitment of all that he is and all that he has to Jesus, then he needs that experience. The date is not important, but a definite commitment of life is of supreme importance.

The devil will bring doubt. If he can get one to doubt this thing, it will hinder him as a witness. Nail this down! John said that the people who have the Son are the ones who have eternal life. It is just this plain: if you have Him, then you have life; if you know in your heart that you have Jesus, then you have life. This is the thing we have to witness in ourselves. I am not trying to put doubt in anybody's mind; I am saying to be sure—know that you have had an experience. Paul said, "For I am confident of this very thing, that He who began a good work in you will perfect it until the day of Christ Jesus" (Philippians 1:6 NASB). Paul said, "For I am convinced that neither death, nor life, nor angels, nor principalities, nor things present, nor things to come, nor powers, nor height, nor depth, nor any other created thing, will be able to separate us from the love of God, which is in Christ Jesus our Lord" (Romans 8:38-39 NASB). "I know," Paul said, "I am persuaded of this." It is a head knowledge, but it is a heart knowledge too. I know in whom I have believed. This is the first thing, personal salvation.

6.B. THE SECOND MUST: DOCTRINAL PERSUASIONS

The soul winner must have some definite persuasions, some definite beliefs. Certain principles are essential; a soul winner must believe them if he is to be effective. These doctrines are the basics of the Christian faith.

6.B.1. THE DIVINE NATURE OF JESUS CHRIST

The witness for Christ must believe the claims of Jesus. Jesus Christ is God's Son. Jesus Christ is God. In order to be effective, the soul winner must believe this. The person who believes that Jesus is just a man, even a good man, will never lead people to commitment to Jesus Christ. One must believe that Jesus Christ is the Son of God. "Simon Peter answered, 'You are the Christ, the Son of the living God.' And Jesus said to him, 'Blessed are you, Simon Barjona, because flesh and blood did not reveal this to you but My Father who is in heaven'" (Matthew 16:16-17 NASB). "The angel answered and said to her, 'The Holy Spirit will come upon you, and the power of the Most High will overshadow you; and for that reason the holy Child shall be called the Son of God" (Luke 1:35 NASB). "And she cried out with a loud voice and said, 'Blessed are you among women, and blessed is the fruit of your womb.' And how has it happened to me, that the mother of my Lord would come to me?" (Luke 1:42-43 NASB).

6.B.2. THE DIVINE INSPIRATION OF THE BIBLE

Paul declared, "All Scripture is inspired by God and profitable for teaching, for reproof, for correction, for training in righteousness" (2 Timothy 3:16 NASB). Peter said, "For no prophecy was ever made by an act of human will, but men moved by the Holy Spirit spoke from God" (2 Peter 1:21 NASB).

My own experience has led me to believe that no substitute exists in personal witnessing for the use of the written Word of God. One may talk to a man and reason with him until he is blue in the face. One can quote Scripture to lost men but will lead very few people to definite commitment to Christ unless he takes the Word of God and shows him in God's Word that he is a sinner who needs to be saved, that he may be saved because Jesus Christ died for him, and he will be saved when he repents and commits his heart and life to Jesus. Use the written Word of God! Now, one will not use it if he doubts the inspiration of the Word of God; the doubter leads very few people to Jesus. An effective soul winner must believe that the Bible is God's Word.

One will not go into battle with a gun that he believes is defective, will he? Would you want to get into a shooting war somewhere as a soldier with a gun that you knew was defective? Neither will the soldier of the Lord if he believes the Sword is defective. He is just not going to use it. The Word of God is the Sword of the Spirit, and it is the Word of God that pierces the human soul. The effective soul winner must be persuaded that the Scriptures are inspired, that the Bible is God's Word.

6.B.3. THE DESTITUTE NATURE OF MAN

The soul winner must believe that man is a sinner. Ample evidence appears in Scripture for this. Jeremiah 17:9 (NASB) states, "The heart is more deceitful than all else And is desperately sick; Who can understand it?" The psalmist said, "Behold, I was brought forth in iniquity, And in sin my mother conceived me" (Psalm 51:5 NASB). Paul declared in Ephesians 2:3, "And were by nature the children of wrath, even as the rest." The preacher said in Ecclesiastes 7:20 (NASB), "Indeed, there is not a righteous man on earth who continually does good and who never sins." Romans 3:10-23 (NASB) deals with it:

As it is written, "There is none righteous, not even one; there is none who understands, there is none who seeks for God; All have turned aside, together they have become useless; there is none who does good, there is not even one. Their throat is an open grave, With their tongues they keep deceiving, the poison of asps is under their lips; whose mouth is full of cursing and bitterness; their feet are swift to shed blood, destruction and misery are in their paths, and the path of peace they have not known,

There is no fear of God before their eyes. Now we know that whatever the Law says, it speaks to those who are under the Law, so that every mouth may be closed and all the world may become accountable to God; because by the works of the Law no flesh will be justified in His sight; for through the Law comes the knowledge of sin. But now apart from the Law the righteousness of God has been manifested, being witnessed by the Law and Prophets, even the righteousness of God through faith in Jesus Christ for all those who believe for there is not distinction; for all have sinned and fall short of the glory of God."

In Mark 10:18 (NASB), Jesus said, "No one is good except God alone." Isaiah wrote in 53:6 (NASB), "All of us like sheep have gone astray, each of us has turned to his own way." The psalmist cried, "The LORD has looked down from heaven upon the sons of men To see if there are any who understand, Who seek after God" (Psalm 14:2-3 NASB). To be an effective soul winner, a person must believe that people are sinners and are lost without Christ.

6.B.4. THE DIVINE WAY OF SALVATION

6.B.4.A. SALVATION IS THROUGH JESUS CHRIST

Peter said, "And there is salvation in no one else; for there is no other name under heaven that has been given among men by which we must be saved" (Acts 4:12 NASB). One must believe that Jesus Christ died for our sins.

Surely our griefs He Himself bore, And our sorrows He carried; Yet we ourselves esteemed Him stricken, Smitten of God, and afflicted. But He was pierced through for our transgressions, He was crushed for our iniquities; The chastening for our well-being fell upon Him, And by His scourging we are healed. All of us like sheep have gone astray, Each of us has turned to his own way; But the LORD has caused the iniquity of us all To fall on Him. (Isaiah 53:4-6 NASB)

"And He Himself bore our sins in His body on the cross, so that we might die to sin and live to righteousness; for by His wounds you were healed" (1 Peter 2:24 NASB). "In Him we have redemption through His blood, the forgiveness of our trespasses, according to the riches of His grace" (Ephesians 1:7 NASB). "And from Jesus Christ, the faithful witness, the firstborn of the dead, and the ruler of the kings of the earth. To Him who loves us and released us from our sins by His blood—and He has made us to be a kingdom, priests to His God and Father—to Him be the glory and the dominion forever and ever. Amen" (Revelation 1:5-6 NASB). A person who does not believe that Jesus alone can save is not going out to tell people that Jesus will save.

6.B.4.B. SALVATION IS BY GRACE ALONE

The soul winner must be persuaded that salvation is by grace alone—not by works, but by grace alone. Paul said in Ephesians 2:8-10 (NASB), "For by grace you have been saved through faith; and that not of yourselves, it is the gift of God; not as a result of works, so that no one may boast. For we are His workmanship, created in Christ Jesus for good works, which God prepared beforehand so that we could walk in them." Notice the order: saved by grace through faith, and then we do good works because we are saved. Romans 3:24 (NASB) states, "Being justified as a gift by His grace through the redemption which is in Christ Jesus." In Romans 4:3-5 (NASB), Paul wrote, "For what does the Scripture say? 'Abraham believed God, and it was credited to Him as righteousness.' Now to the one who works, his wage is credited as a favor, but as what is due. But to the one who does not work, but believes in Him who justifies the ungodly, his faith is credited as righteousness." Paul wrote in Titus 3:5 (NASB), "He saved us, not on the basis of deeds which we have done in righteousness, but according to His mercy, by the washing of regeneration and renewing by the Holy Spirit." Paul said, "How I did not shrink from declaring to you anything that was profitable, and teaching you publicly and from house to house, solemnly testifying to both Jews and Greeks of repentance toward God and faith in our Lord Jesus Christ" (Acts 20:20-21 NASB). Salvation is by grace alone, through faith—in other words, through commitment of life to Jesus Christ.

6.B.5. THE IMMINENT RETURN OF THE LORD JESUS

The effective soul winner is one who is definitely persuaded of the doctrine of the Lord's return. Jesus is coming back again. Here is a great incentive to witness. If we believe Jesus is coming, if we are really looking for Him to come, if we can call for the return of Jesus as John did, we will be soul winners. If you thought Jesus was coming today, wouldn't you rather lead somebody to the Lord than anything else?

6.C. THE THIRD MUST: PERSONAL PURITY

We have mentioned *personal salvation*, *persuasions* of the soul winner, and now, *purity* of the soul winner. If a person is going to bring people to Jesus, he must live what he talks. Guy King said we ought to walk what we talk. The soul winner must be pure, he must have a holy life. He has to have a saved soul, and he must have a redeemed life, if he is going to be effective. Now, the message of the gospel is of supreme importance. But how much more effective is the message if it is given through a redeemed messenger—that is, one whose life is redeemed. Paul, in Romans 12:1 (NASB), talked about our obligation as children of God. He said, "Therefore I urge you, brethren, by the mercies of God, to present your bodies a living and holy sacrifice, acceptable to God, which is your spiritual service of worship." We should present our bodies to the Lord as holy sacrifices. In 2 Corinthians 6:17 (NASB), Paul said, "'Therefore, come out from their midst and be separate,' says the Lord. 'And do not touch what is unclean; and I will welcome you.'"

Paul in Hebrews said, "Therefore, since we have so great a cloud of witnesses surrounding us, let us lay aside every encumbrance and the sin which so easily entangles us, and let us run with endurance the race that is set before us" (Hebrews 12:1 NASB).

The sin in our lives, the sin that surrounds us, the sin that is tempting to us, must be laid aside if we are to run the Christian life as we ought to run. The soul winner needs to live a pure life, a holy life.

6.D. THE FOURTH MUST: A SENSE OF DIVINE PURPOSE IN LIFE

The soul winner must have one overriding purpose in his life. And that one purpose is obedience to Christ. This has already been said many times, but it needs to be said again, that the real measuring stick of the Christian is obedience. The soul winner, to be effective, must have one over-riding purpose in his life, and that is obedience to Christ. When one has for his purpose in his life obedience to Christ, he will be an effective soul winner. What is the purpose of our lives anyway? Is it obedience? Jesus said, "You did not choose Me but I chose you, and appointed you that you would go and bear fruit, and that your fruit would remain, so that whatever you ask of the Father in My name He may give to you" (John 15:16 NASB). Jesus chose us; we did not choose Him. He appointed us to go and bear fruit. This is our business—to be obedient to Him. We should make clear our primary duty, our primary purpose. Paul said to Timothy in 2 Timothy 4:1-2 (NASB), "I solemnly charge you in the presence of God and of Christ Jesus, who is to judge the living and the dead, and by His appearing and His kingdom: preach the word; be ready in season and out of season; reprove, rebuke, exhort, with great patience and instruction." *Be obedient to Christ*, Paul is saying to Timothy.

I read an interesting story about Jerome, the great scholar, who translated the Bible into Latin.[28] Jerome supposedly had a dream one night and saw himself standing before the judgment seat of Christ. The Lord on His throne said to him, "Who art thou?" He answered, "Jerome, a Christian." A stern voice from the throne said, "It is false! Thou art no Christian, but a Ciceronian; for where your treasure is there will your heart be also." Jerome woke up and then prayed that God would forgive him for loving his books so much that they kept him from being the soul winner that he ought to be, that they kept him from having the love that he ought to have for the people for whom Christ died. This is a peril that faces every one of us. When we are involved in academic life, the danger that we will love the books too much can be present. We must study, but we must not get so wrapped up in book study that we forget the reason we are studying those books. The overriding purpose in every life ought to be obedience to Christ.

John Wesley, in his *Twelve Rules* for Methodist preachers (I think he spoke for Baptist preachers too) said, "You have nothing to do but save souls. Therefore, spend and be spent in this work. It is not your business to preach so many times, but to save as many souls as you can; to bring as many sinners as you can to repentance, and with all your power build them up in that holiness without which they cannot see the Lord."[29] That is our business. Our business is not to preach twice on Sunday and speak at prayer meetings on Wednesday nights. It is to reach people for Christ and build them up in the life of holiness.

Richard Baxter, a great English preacher, many years ago said, "It is an ill sign of a false, self-seeking heart that can be content to be still doing and see no fruit of their labors."[30] It is nothing to brag about if you work somewhere three or four years and don't see anybody saved. It is not a matter to brag about, it is a matter to pray about. One can't always judge the success of the ministry by the number of people who are baptized. There has been an over emphasis on numbers sometimes, but every number represents a person, and our business is to reach people for Christ.

6.E. THE FIFTH MUST: PASSION FOR THE LOST

Jesus wept over the lost multitudes. He cried literal tears. Paul in Hebrews said that Jesus, during His earthly ministry, "offered up prayers and supplications with strong crying and tears. . ." (Hebrews 5:7 KJV). Jesus looked down on Jerusalem and said, "Jerusalem, Jerusalem, who kills the prophets and stones those who are sent to her! How often I wanted to gather your children together, the way a hen gathers her chicks under her wings, and you were unwilling" (Matthew 23:37 NASB). Jesus cried over lost people. Compassion led to passion in the life of Jesus. There must, if we are going to be effective soul winners, be passion in our lives. Jesus said, "Because lawlessness is increased, most people's love will grow cold" (Matthew 24:12 NASB). Jesus implied in His Word to the church at Ephesus (Revelation 2) that this was their trouble. You must come back to your first love, come back to the first things, get back to the primary things. Have you ever wept over lost people in your community, I mean really wept? Have you become so burdened that you cried because of a lost person? It is not difficult to cry about a child who is ill, it is not difficult to cry about a loved one who dies physically, is it? But, have you ever wept over your loved ones and your friends who are dead spiritually? A broken heart lends passion to the soul-winner's pleading.

Some years ago, a church which is very dear to my heart had in its bulletin a record of the number of baptisms for several years. One paragraph bragged about the number of people who had been baptized. I knew the church well enough to know how many resident members they had, and I figured that it took thirty-five of them that year to win one person to Jesus. That is nothing to brag about!

A large percentage of churches in the Southern Baptist Convention last year did not baptize anybody the whole year. This must be true in other denominations too. Something is wrong with those preachers or their sermons. Preaching may fail and singing may fail, but individual concern doesn't fail. If you care enough to weep over people individually and personally and keep on going because you care, you are going to reach people for Christ. If the people in these thousands of churches had really cared, somebody would have been saved. It is not that people are not lost in these communities. We need to have a passion for souls, or we will never be effective as soul winners.

George Whitefield, a powerful English preacher of the gospel, was preaching once in Edinburgh. He was preaching early in the morning before people went to work, and people were getting up early to come and hear him preach. A man on his way to hear Whitefield preach one day met the agnostic Scottish philosopher David Hume. Hume was on his way to hear Whitefield, and the man said to him, "I didn't think you believed in the gospel." Hume replied, "I don't, but Whitefield does." If you have passion in your heart, they will listen to you.[31]

People know that you care if you talk to them about Jesus. A lost man said to a preacher one day, "You may talk to me because I believe you care whether I am saved or not." He said to this preacher, "Don't you let so and so ever come back and talk to me again, because it is a profession with him. He doesn't care whether I am saved or lost, he wants to baptize me as a statistic into his church." Now that is a severe condemnation.

Compassion—care for the soul. This is the thing which above all is needed in us. Somebody asked recently how you stir up compassion and get this passion. This person said, "I had it one time and I haven't had it for a long time, and I want a real passion for souls." George Sweazey, in *Effective Evangelism*, spoke about this. He said,

The heartbeat does not pick up until after exercise has started. The power of the Holy Spirit does not come to those who with folded hands are looking toward heaven waiting for a visitation, but to those whose hands have taken up some work that is too big for them. Apparently His power only flows in where there is some chance for it to flow out. Our souls do not grow through spiritual exercises alone, but through spiritual exercises made necessary by the urgency of some great task. Jesus may have meant the order to be significant when He said, "Take my yoke upon you and learn of me" (Matthew 11:29).[32]

Go to work and learn of me. Think about that. The way to arouse passion for souls is to go out and start witnessing to them, asking the Lord to help as you witness. The Great Commission of Jesus is to go and make disciples of all nations. He said, "Lo, I am with you." That word *go* in the Great Commission is a participle, *going,* or *as you go, make disciples and lo, I am with you as you go.* When we go out with a passion for lost souls, then we will be going as obedient Christians. Dr. J. H. Jowett said a church will call a minister, place him in a refrigerator, and expect him to sweat. But the best thing to do if you are in a cold place is to exercise. That will get you warm. So, if you get in a cold church, go to work. Work up a sweat. The only way we will ever change our churches from these cold, dead things that we know, to the warm, alive, soul-winning churches that we long to know, is for those of us who lead them to show them the way. Passion. The following poem is worth thinking about.

> *Would you care if some friend you had met day by day*
> *Should never be told about Jesus?*
> *Are you willing that he in the Judgment should say*
> *"No one ever told me of Jesus?"*
> —Author Unknown

Do you read those books about the great evangelists and the time of great evangelization? Have you read of the people holding to the pews in fear of sliding into hell, and of people crying out because they were under a conviction of sin? Have you ever wondered why we don't see anything like that in our day? Maybe the reason is a lack of passion in the hearts of preachers. Samuel May, Jr. said to William Lloyd Garrison, "Oh, my friend, do try to keep more cool, you are all on fire." Garrison said to him, "I have a need to be all on fire—I have mountains of ice around me to melt."[33] Passion. Passion wins. Real heart concern, real heart burden for people, wins people. People know if you care. It is our business to care. We are supposed to deal with the intellect and the emotion to move the will, but our purpose is to move the will. Too long have we talked about hardened sinners and difficult cases. It is time for us to get a little passion in our souls and go out there and tell them about Jesus, to let them know we care. Love melt hearts, passion melts people.

6.F. THE SIXTH MUST: PRAYER

Let me commend a book to you: E. M. Bounds, *Power in Prayer*. Prayer undergirds and prepares us for all we do for the Savior. If you don't have any passion in your heart, pray that God will give you a burden for somebody. People get saved when somebody gets a burden. One called of God must pray. Moses cried out to the Lord, "I alone am not able to carry all this people, because it is too burdensome for me" (Numbers 11:14 NASB). If one is a Christian, no matter how limited his opportunities to witness, it is too heavy for him, and he must pray. Will you pray,

> God help me to see in those I meet
> On country road or city street
> Not just people passing by
> But those for whom Jesus came to die.
> —Author Unknown

6.G. THE SEVENTH MUST: SPIRITUAL POWER

Paul said, "For our gospel did not come to you in word only, but also in power and in the Holy Spirit and with full conviction; just as you know what kind of men we proved to be among you for your sake" (1 Thessalonians 1:5 NASB). If one is going to witness and win people to Christ, he needs power. Only once source of power is there for the Christian, and that power is the Spirit of God. No greater truth can be found in all the Word of God than this: "'Not by might nor by power, but by My Spirit,' says the LORD of hosts" (Zechariah 4:6 NASB).

The power of the Spirit of God is necessary if one is to witness effectively. This should possibly be first on the list, and yet it sums it all up, does it not? All of those who have the power of the Spirit will have all these other things that they need. However, one cannot fill a life that is already full. If your life is filled with sin and self, you will not be filled with the Spirit. But, if you will pray to God, He will empty you and then He will fill you. Paul said, "I have been crucified with Christ; and it is no longer I who live, but Christ lives in me; and the life which I now live in the flesh I live by faith in the Son of God, who loved me and gave Himself up for me" (Galatians 2:20 NASB). Paul was saying, "Paul is dead—Paul doesn't live here anymore. Jesus Christ lives in this body." If one is filled with the Spirit, he will win souls to Christ.

In these days, with so much misunderstanding about the Holy Spirit, a great need calls us to return to the Scriptures. This Spirit is come to glorify Jesus—not to glorify the person who is filled with the Spirit, but to glorify Jesus. "And He, when He comes . . . will glorify Me" (John 16:8, 14 NASB). The Spirit has come to testify of Jesus. Jesus said, "But when the Comforter is come . . . he shall testify of me" (John 15:26 KJV). The person who is filled with the Spirit brings people to Jesus. He does not attract attention to himself or to the Spirit, he attracts attention to Jesus. Praise God for anything that happens in your life that will glorify Jesus. Thank God for anything that happens in your life that testifies of Jesus and brings people to Him. But be wary of anything other than Jesus Christ. Paul's word to the Ephesians is a good word to the soul winner: "Be filled with the Spirit" (Ephesians 5:18 KJV). Power is a must for the soul winner, and the source of power is the Spirit of God.

6.H. THE EIGHTH MUST: PERSEVERANCE

When we ask what the Lord requires of us, the answer is that we are to go to every person with the gospel. As we go, we know that many, though they hear and go on hearing, will not understand (Matthew 13:13-15 KJV). If we ask, as did Isaiah, "How long, O Lord?," we may hear the answer that Isaiah received (words which are particularly ominous in our own day): "Until the cities are devastated and without inhabitant . . . And the land is utterly desolate" (Isaiah 6:11 NASB).

It is said that Dr. Oswald Chambers visited a dying infidel in Glasgow twenty-one times and was refused admission every time. But at the twenty-second visit, the infidel invited him in. He wanted to see the man who could be refused twenty-one times and still come back again! And then Dr. Chambers had a chance to tell the dying man of Him who can save. What if he had not yielded to the Spirit of God who would not let him cease from going?

Do the demons of hell know you as a faithful witness for Christ? Oh, that the demons might say of us what one of their number said of Paul: "Jesus I know and Paul I know" (Acts 19:15 KJV).

CHAPTER 7

THE SOUL-WINNER'S METHOD

7.A. SOME WORDS OF ADVICE ON EVANGELISM

Some things are essential to do, if we are to be effective witnesses for the Lord. The first of the dos is the following:

7.A.1. DO CLAIM GOD'S PROMISE OF WISDOM

God's Word says, "Those who have insight will shine brightly like the brightness of the expanse of heaven, and those who lead the many to righteousness, like the stars forever and ever" (Daniel 12:3 NASB). "He that winneth souls is wise" (Proverbs 11:30 KJV). None of us is wise enough to lead somebody else to Christ without God's help. We need to be conscious of that. It does not matter how much education one has; how many places one has been; how many people one has talked with; how many sermons one has preached or heard; none of us is wise enough in his own wisdom to lead somebody else to Christ. But listen to James 1:5. God promises us something. James said, "But if any of you lacks wisdom, let him ask of God, who gives to all generously and without reproach, and it will be given to him" (James 1:5 NASB). Let me give you the Allison translation of it: "If any man needs wisdom, let him ask God for it, and He will give him all he needs, and won't fuss at him for asking." You see, God wants us to be wise in the most important thing in the world—helping people come to know Jesus. So, in the very beginning, do claim God's promise of wisdom. Ask God to help you say the right thing, at the right time, in the right way. Claim God's promise of wisdom.

7.A.2. DO CLAIM GOD'S PROMISE OF DELIVERANCE FROM FEAR

Why is it that most of God's people never take the Word of God and witness to lost people and lead them to Christ? Obviously most of us do not, if it takes one hundred Christians one whole year to win somebody to Christ. Some answers could be, "We don't have confidence in ourselves." "We're just not interested enough." "We don't take time." "We don't remember that God said put first things first." I believe real Christians want to put first things first. But I believe the main reason Christian people do not really witness is *fear*. Are we not afraid that we will not do it right? That goes back to a lack of confidence. We are afraid we will say the wrong thing or that we will do the wrong thing. We are afraid that somebody will laugh at us; we are afraid that somebody will not understand; we are afraid we will drive a person farther away. (And by the way, that is one of the devil's lies that he has used on us over and over: "Oh, listen, you'll push him farther away." When a man is lost, he is about as far away from God as he can get. The devil has carried some folks down to hell with him, convincing Christian people not to talk to them because we might push them farther away. That is the devil's strategy).

We are afraid. But who is the author of fear? The devil is! God is not the author of fear, is He? Paul said, "For God has not given us a spirit of timidity, but of power and love and discipline" (2 Timothy 1:7 NASB). King David said, "I sought the LORD, and He answered me, And delivered me from all my fears" (Psalm 34:4 NASB). Now, if He will do that for David, will He do it for every one of His children? Yes! Do claim God's promise of deliverance from fear, for, "God is faithful, who will not allow you to be tempted beyond what you are able, but with the temptation will provide the way of escape also, so that you will be able to endure it" (1 Corinthians 10:13 NASB).

We are dealing with eternity. Do not let fear conquer you. Turn it over to God. Call on Him and ask Him to deliver you from fear. Then trust Him to do it! "There is no fear in love; but perfect love casts out fear, because fear involves punishment, and the one who fears is not perfected in love" (1 John 4:18 NASB).

7.A.3. DO WATCH FOR OPPORTUNITIES TO WITNESS

Oh, people all around us are lost. Many people say, "I don't know any lost people." But they're all around us! How about the pharmacist or the checker at the store? You may say, "Well, they are working, and I don't want to bother them." I spoke to a group of ladies in a little town in North Louisiana about witnessing, and they went and shared the gospel with their hairdresser. She accepted Christ that day! Her house was next door to the church, and she had been fixing the hair of many of the women in the church for two years. But nobody had ever talked to her before about the Savior. It had never occurred to them that she might be lost. They were not thinking in terms of people, you see. Opportunities are present all around us.

7.A.4. DO GO AS A FRIEND WHO HAS SOMETHING GOOD TO SHARE

Take a tip from a good salesperson. Do salespeople begin by wringing their hands and saying, "I don't know if you want to buy anything." No, they believe that you have a need and that they have the best product in the business, and they can help you get it. We are not selling anything, but we have the most wonderful thing in the world—eternal life, as the gift from God. And every person in this world needs Jesus. Let us not mumble and wring our hands and apologize for going to tell people about Jesus.

Let me ask you something. Who is the best friend you have? Is it Jesus? Is He really your best friend? Who is the best friend anybody can have? Jesus! Do you believe that? Why apologize and why beat around the bush? Why wring your hands, and why hesitate to introduce people to the best friend they will ever have? He is the one friend everybody in the whole world needs. Do go as a friend who has something good to share.

7.A.5. DO DEAL WITH ONLY ONE SOUL AT A TIME

It is better to talk with the prospect alone, if possible. If it is impossible, witness to as many as there are in the room. If you go to talk to a father and mother and two teenage children, and they are all lost, witness to one of them at a time. Try to lead that one through a decision, then turn to the next one. Lead that one through the plan of salvation.

Gray Allison related this story: "Recently, we led a father, a mother, a sixteen-year-old son, and a fourteen-year-old daughter to Christ in one afternoon in the same living room. We had the joy of seeing them come that night, all four of them, to make their public confession of faith. But if we had tried to lead them all to the Lord at the same time, the chances are we would not have led any of them to Christ. Lead one person to a decision for Christ and then turn to the others."

7.A.6. DO LET ONE PERSON AT A TIME WITNESS WITHOUT INTERRUPTION

If you go out with a partner, in twos, determine before you get to the place of witness who is going to begin the witness. If your partner is to be the witness, pray for your witnessing partner and do not interrupt him when he is witnessing. You may harm the witnessing opportunity. Let him witness. Have a prearranged signal if you are to begin talking. Let him give you a signal if he wants you to take over the witness. For instance, he could say, "Brother Gray may want to say something." But do not interrupt when someone else is witnessing.

7.A.7. DO AVOID ARGUMENT

This principle should be put in neon lights! Gray Allison and a pastor visited a mother of two children. She had been a Roman Catholic but was excommunicated by her church because she had married outside the church. She could not take the sacraments. She did not have any church to call home, but her heart was spiritually hungry, and it showed. She did not know anything about Baptists except bad things, because that is all that she had ever been told. We began to talk with her, and that preacher took out his Bible and almost literally beat her over the head with it. He backed her into a corner. Every time she said something, he would argue and give her a verse of Scripture. He won the argument, because she really did not know anything about spiritual matters. But, oh, we did not win her to Christ! We left her there with her heart still hungry and her life still empty.

Nobody has ever been argued into the kingdom of God. You may win the argument, but you will lose the soul. Just do not argue. Remember, you are there to show him from the Word of God that he is a sinner who needs to be saved, that he may be saved because Jesus died for him, and he can be saved through repentance and faith. Stay on the main track, but do not argue.

7.A.8. DO SHOW PATIENCE

Many times, a person can give you a reason to be impatient. People may say some awfully bad things, but if you show impatience, you are going to lose the patient. One cannot always be patient, but he can avoid showing his impatience. You have to remember what you are there for. Remember, too, that dead people do not get their feelings hurt. And, if we are in Christ, we are dead to self. If you are dead to sin and self, so that Christ lives in you, you can sit there and listen to anything, yet love the person and tell him in love what he needs to know.

7.A.9. DO REMEMBER WE DO NOT FAIL IF WE WITNESS

Who wins people to Christ? The Holy Spirit does! Nail that down—the Holy Spirit wins people to Christ. What are we supposed to do? Witness! Now, when do we fail? When we do not witness! If we could ever get that straight, it would take care of a lot of our fears. We are not supposed to win them—that is the work of the Holy Spirit. We are to witness to them with the Word of God in love so that the Holy Spirit can take the Word of God and bring conviction and conversion. The tragedy is that a person goes out and tries one time, the one witnessed to does not trust the Lord, and the witness says, "I told you Gray Allison wasn't telling me the truth. He said anybody who loves Jesus can bring others to Him. And you see, I failed. I just can't do it." He turns away discouraged and never tries again. But you do not fail if you witness. The Holy Spirit must win the soul—we are to witness. Oh, if we'd remember that!

An old deacon in a church in Mississippi became angry at a preacher because he preached that one cannot be happy if he is not obedient, and one is not obedient until he becomes a witness for Christ. He said, "I just can't stand that. That upsets me. I can't witness!" He was seventy-five years old. But he came to the witnessing class because he felt that as a deacon he had to come. Then he committed himself to witness because it was required of those in the class. One day he came, disturbed, and said, "Preacher, you must help me. I've been witnessing to a man but haven't been able to bring him to commitment to Christ—you must come help me." The pastor went with him and they led a seventy-two-year-old man to Jesus. The deacon asked to have a word on Saturday night at the witnessing class. He said, "You know, I got so angry at the preacher on this thing, and he made me come. I felt that I had to do it." Then he smiled and said, "I'm glad he did. When I was twenty-five years old, I went out and tried to lead a man to Christ. He didn't trust the Lord, and I knew right then I couldn't do it and I never did try again, until this week." Fifty years of wasted life! He thought he had failed. Oh, don't be discouraged by apparent failure. You do what you're supposed to do—witness with the Word of God in love—and God's Holy Spirit will do what He's supposed to do. You'll see folks saved.

7.B. HOW TO MAKE THE APPROACH

How does one make an approach to a lost person so he can use the Word of God in witnessing? It cannot be said too often that no substitute exists for the use of the written Word of God in witnessing. This does not mean that the Bible is a charm or something magic, but it does something to a person to see written down in God's Word the truth about himself, his need, what can be done about it, and how to do it. I have tried witnessing every way that I know, and nothing is as effective as sitting down with a man to show him in God's Word what God says. So, use a Bible or a New Testament in witnessing.

Let's talk about how to begin the interview so that we can take the Word of God and show a person in the Word of God that he is a sinner who needs to be saved; that he may be saved; and how to be saved. Here are several approaches that you can use to begin a witnessing conversation.

7.B.1. APOLOGIZE FOR NOT WITNESSING

If you have a friend or a loved one and you have never really witnessed to that person with the written Word of God, this can be an excellent way to make the approach. Suppose his name is Jim. Go to Jim's house, knock on the door. When he comes to the door, you may say, "Jim, I've come over to apologize to you." He likely will say, "Well, what in the world for?" You say, "We've hunted together, and we've fished together, we've been places together, we've talked about everything in the world, but I've never really talked to you about the most important thing in the world. I'd like to do that. May I come in?" What do you think he will say? "Surely, come on in." You don't need another approach. Just start right there and say, "Jim, the most important thing in the world is a man's relationship to God. I brought my New Testament over here, and I want to talk with you about your relationship to God." Then start witnessing.

That is the best approach I know, because it's an honest approach. If you have been with a person, if you know a person, if you love that person, and if you've never witnessed to that person with the written Word of God, you do owe him an apology. You have wronged him, if you have known him for years and you have never witnessed to him with the written Word of God. Inviting him to church is not enough. Many people in our world do not really know that they need to be saved. They do not know how to be saved. So go over there and say, "I've come to apologize." That will open the door.

7.B.2. MAKE A FRIENDLY VISIT

Another method which has been proven successful is to go as a friend with something good to share. It works with a person you know well, or a person you have never seen before. Knock on the door and say, "I'm Gray Allison from First Baptist Church and am out visiting for our church. Could I come in and visit with you a few minutes?" Most people will say, "Surely, come on in." Go in, sit down, and start a friendly conversation. Remember, if you are not careful, the conversation will stay casual. You'll visit for an hour with that person and talk about football or the weather or business. Then you'll look at your watch, and you will say, "Well, my goodness, I've been here an hour and it's time for me to go." You will get up and as you start out, you'll say, "I surely wish you'd come down and visit us at the church sometimes." Now that is not witnessing. It is better than nothing, but it is not witnessing. Go in and begin a casual conversation. Get on a friendly basis with him, but do not let it stay casual. You can start anywhere in any conversation and use four simple statements:

1. *"Jim, have you been thinking much lately about spiritual things?"* You see, it doesn't matter what you are talking about. You can just start, "Jim, have you been thinking about spiritual things?" Now, here is the beauty of the question. You see, if he says yes, you can say, "Wonderful!" and go to the second thing. If he says no, you can still go right to the second thing. "Have you been thinking much lately about spiritual things?" Whatever he answers, you can go immediately to the second thing.

2. *"What would you say is a person's greatest spiritual need?"* Or *"What would you say a person ought to have more than anything else in the way of spiritual things?"* Say it the way you want to say it. Now he may say, "Well, he needs to be a good man." Or he may say, "Well, a fellow ought to go to church." Sometimes, but not often, a lost person will say, "A man needs to be saved." Whatever he says, you can go immediately to the third thing.

3. *"The Bible says it is a salvation experience. Have you ever had a definite experience with Christ?"* Now notice what was said: "Have you been thinking much lately about spiritual things?" Almost everybody has. "What would you say is a person's greatest spiritual need? The Bible says it is a salvation experience. Have you had a definite experience with Christ sometime in the past?" Notice that you did not say, "Are you a Christian?" What will a man say if you ask him this? He probably will say, "Yes, I am." You see, many people do not know what a Christian is. Many church members assume that they are Christians because their family are Christians. Some people believe that they are Christians because they are Americans, and America is supposedly a Christian nation. Therefore, they reason, if one is an American, he is supposed to be a Christian.

   Now, don't ask him, "Are you a Christian?" If you ask that down in South Louisiana, where I lived for eleven years, a man will say, "Yes, I'm a Catholic," and you're through with him right there. Instead, say, "Have you had a definite experience with Christ sometime in the past?" Now, suppose he says yes to that question, what would you say? "Wonderful, tell me about it!" I like to hear peoples' experiences with the Lord, don't you? Don't you like to hear people tell about what Jesus did for them? "That's wonderful, Jim, tell me about it." But suppose he cannot tell you about a definite experience. Note, some people may say yes just to get rid of you; this is how the devil works. If you say, "Have you followed through with it?" He may say yes or no or something else. You should say, "Tell me about it." Now, if he cannot tell you about a definite experience with Christ, go to the fourth thing.

4. *"May I talk with you about this for a few minutes?"* If he says "No" when you ask if he has had a definite experience with Christ, go to the fourth thing, "May I talk with you about this for a few minutes?" If he says, "Well, I'm not sure," or, "I hope I have," or something else, say, "May I talk with you about this for a few minutes?" Notice that there is just no way to get off the track. You move right through and are down to the interview. "Have you been thinking much lately about spiritual things? What would you say is a person's greatest spiritual need? The Bible says it is a salvation experience. Have you had a definite experience with Christ sometime in the past? May I talk with you about this a few minutes?" What do you think he will say? "Why, certainly." This will work almost every time you try it. When you say, "May I talk with you about this a few minutes?" reach for your New Testament. Do not hesitate at all. Start right then. Say, "God says in the Bible . . ." and deal with those Scriptures. Learn those four simple things. They are not hard to learn. One can learn them in a matter of minutes.

7.B.3. ILLUSTRATION ABOUT MEDICAL CARE

Let me give you another approach that will work. Do you know anyone who has never been to a doctor? Most of us have been to a doctor at some time. When you are sick and you go to the doctor, what is the first thing the doctor tries to do? He tries to find out what is wrong with you. He diagnoses your case, and then what does he do? He prescribes for you, tells you what to do about it, and tells you how to do it. But a doctor never ties you down on a table, props your mouth open, and pours the medicine down you whether you want it or not. So, when you are trying to witness, go to the person and say, "Jim" (you can be in a casual conversation), "did you ever go to a doctor?" And he'll say, "Well, surely." "What's the first thing the doctor does?" Get him to tell you that the doctor finds out what's wrong with him and tells him what to do about it, and how to do it, and get him to say that the doctor never has forced him to take the medicine. But he knows what's wrong, he knows what to do about it, and he knows how to do it—it's up to him to take the medicine if he wants to get well. Then say, "Jim, that is what God tells us in the Bible. God tells us what is wrong with every one of us. He tells us what to do about it, He tells us how to do it, but He never makes us do it. It is up to us to do the thing which will make us right with Him. God tells us in Romans 3:10 (NASB), 'As it is written, There is none righteous, not even one.'" Then you are ready to proceed. You tell him from God's Word what's wrong with him, tell him what God has done about it, tell him how to be right with God. That is not hard to remember, because we've all had the experience of going to a doctor.

Many ways exist to begin a conversation so that without embarrassment to yourself or the other person one can take the Word of God and show him in the Word of God that he needs to be saved, that he may be saved, and how to be saved.

7.B.4. THE OBJECT METHOD

Another way to witness is with the *object method*. Jesus used this method with the woman at the well. The experience is recorded in the fourth chapter of John. Jesus, tired and hot, came to the well and sat to rest. The Samaritan woman came to draw water. Jesus said to her, "Give me a drink of water." Now, there is nothing that seems more normal than that—He was thirsty, hot, and tired, and He asked for a drink of water. But the woman was a Samaritan, Jesus was a Jew, and this started the conversation. Through this simple request for a drink of water, He was able to talk to her about the water of life, the water which if a person drinks he will never thirst again. And she came to know Jesus.

It is worth our noting here that Jesus did not cultivate this woman. He did not know her, and she did not know Him until they met there at the well. He led her to a commitment to Him right there. If we have the love of God in our hearts and we love lost people, we will give them the Word of God. God will save some of them. Some may say that is not the right way to do it. Read the New Testament and see how many times this very sort of thing was done in New Testament times by Jesus and the disciples.

Another way to use the object method as a beginning is to talk about the weather. I used this once in Pennsylvania while it was snowing. I began talking with the person and said to her, "Isn't this a beautiful day?" She said, "You just came in out of it; you know it is snowing out there. The weather is terrible!" I said, "Yes, but God's Word says, 'This is the day which the Lord has made; Let us rejoice and be glad in it' (Psalm 118:24 NASB). It is a good day because God made it. You know, the Bible says so many wonderful things. The Bible tells us . . . ."

A preacher and I were in Alabama one Saturday afternoon, and we drove up to a man's house to witness. He had been witnessed to a number of times. We drove around to the back because it was raining. It was one of those Alabama gully-washers! The water was running across the backyard over a foot deep. We took off our shoes and socks, rolled up our trouser legs, and walked through the water to the back porch. We found a deacon sitting at the dining room table witnessing to this man. That man was saved that day, and the thing that impressed him was that people would care enough about him to come in that kind of weather just to talk to him about Jesus. That was a perfect opportunity to use the approach, "Isn't it a beautiful day? God says, 'This is the day the Lord hath made, Let us rejoice and be glad in it' (Psalm 118:24 NASB). Doesn't God say wonderful things in His Word? He tells us in the Bible many wonderful things, and He tells us that we all have a need because we are sinners."

One may use the pencil and eraser method—this is a good object lesson. This is good to use if you don't know this person and he doesn't know you. Ask him if you have the correct information about his address, etc. Take a card, put down his name and address, etc. Make a mistake (on purpose), and erase it. Make another mistake and erase it. Then say, "Aren't erasers wonderful things? If you make a mistake you can just erase it and start all over again. Don't you wish we could do that with our lives? Don't you wish you could just erase the past with all the mistakes and start over again?" Now, who doesn't wish that? You can say to him, "You know, you can do that!" Tell them what the Bible says and then begin the witness.

7.B.5. BEGIN A CASUAL CONVERSATION

Another method of beginning the interview is to just begin a casual conversation and watch for an opening. You will find sometimes as you are talking that the person will open the door for the Bible witness. Do not be in any hurry, and be a good listener. If you listen to him, out of courtesy he will listen to you. Keep your ears open, listening to detect a tender spot or tender memory. Many times, in a conversation, you will find a tender spot or a tender memory that will open the door.

Sometime ago I was in a town in Louisiana. The pastor was tied up in some work at the church and could not visit and witness as we had planned to do. He asked me if I would mind going by myself, and I said no, I didn't mind. I went to a home where the woman was a Christian and a member of that church. Her husband was not a Christian. His background was Church of Christ. He had been an oil field worker all his life and had lived in that town for twenty-eight years. I knocked on the door, and when he came to the door, I introduced myself. He said, "Yeah, I know who you are—I've seen your pictures on the posters." He knew who I was, and he was expecting the preachers to come since they always did during a revival. (That leads me to put in a little "lagniappe" here—[Editor's Note: a small aside comment].—If we will witness to them between revivals, we will win them. Surprise one of them and go see them the week after the revival and witness to him).

Well, he was expecting me and the other preacher. I asked him if I could come in, and he said, "Yes, I will be glad for you to come." He was really nervous! I started trying to talk to him, and he fended me off. (He had gotten pretty expert at it after fifty-eight years. He knew how to close the doors just as quickly as I could open them). So we sat there and talked and drank three or four cups of that good South Louisiana coffee, but I could not get the door opened. Every time I started one approach, he would shut the door. But as we talked on, I said, "Where are you from?"

He said, "Right here."

I said, "I was born in Gilliam, Louisiana." (That doesn't mean a thing to you, but Gilliam is twelve miles from Ida, and Ida is my birthplace.) I said, "Man, that is home, that is in the pine hill country!"

His face brightened up, and we began to talk about people we knew who lived in those towns and in between. The wall of resistance began to crumble. I said, "Where did you go to church when you lived in Gilliam?"

He said, "Church of Christ."

"Oh, are you a member of the Church of Christ?"

He answered, "No, but my mother and daddy were."

"Then your mother and daddy were Christians?"

He hit the coffee table with his big fist and said, "If anybody in this world was a Christian, my mother was!" Now, he gave me a key word. What is the key word? *Was*. Oh, listen and keep your ears open. "If anybody in this world was a Christian, my mother *was*." She is dead—this is what he was saying.

I said, "Your mother is not living anymore?"

He replied, "No, my mother and daddy are both dead."

"If your mother and daddy were both Christians, they have gone to heaven to be with the Lord, haven't they?"

He said, "Yes, sir, if anybody ever went to heaven, my mother did."

I said, "I know that you want to go to heaven too, to be with your mother, don't you?"

He said, "I surely do."

Then I asked, "Could I tell you how to get there?"

And he said, "I wish you would."

In about twenty minutes, he was on his way to heaven. There was a tender spot there. His mother had known and loved Jesus, she was dead, and she was in heaven. This was his belief. He loved his mother, and this led him to love his mother's Lord. If you will keep your ears opened when you are talking to people, they will show you a tender spot or a tender memory.

I was out talking to a young couple not long ago, and right in the middle of our conversation this lady said, "Brother Allison, what happens when a baby dies? Where does a baby go?" What was she saying to me? She was saying that she had lost a baby. I turned to 2 Samuel, chapter 12, and told her about David's experience when his baby died. David said, "I shall go to him, but he shall not return to me" (verse 23 KJV). I told her that a baby who dies goes to be with the Lord. Then I said, "I know that you want to go to heaven too." She did want to, and she is going, because that opened the door for witnessing.

Perhaps someone will say, "You are playing on people's emotions." I am not playing on them but dealing with them. One cannot love without emotion. People have both intellect and emotion. Intellect and emotion together will move the will. That is what we are trying to do—to move the will to be surrendered to Jesus. That mother's heart was broken because her baby died. She was grieving, she needed somebody to help her, she needed Jesus. Use experiences like that to help a mother come to know the best friend she will ever have in this world or the next. Give her an assurance that she will be with that baby one day.

We ought to never take advantage of a person. But you are not taking advantage of a person if you are introducing him to Jesus. You are helping him to experience the best thing that will ever happen to him. He will thank you not just for a lifetime, he will thank you for eternity that he has come to know Jesus. He is not going to meet you on the streets in heaven and say, "You surely took advantage of me down there!" He will stand in the presence of the Lord and thank you for coming to talk to him about Jesus.

7.B.6. AN EMPLOYMENT ILLUSTRATION

Again, use the person's vocation, the way they make a living. For example, you can use the occupation of being an accountant. In talking to an accountant, talk to him about his work, about how the debit and credit side must balance. There can't be any difference; they must balance. Say to him, "You know God says that our books must balance. One of these days we are going to stand before God, and He is going to balance the books." Use Romans 14:10-12 (Allison translation), "We shall all give account of ourselves unto God. . . ." You can then say, "God is going to draw the double line one of these days, and the books must balance. We can't balance our own books, can we?" You can start there. This is a good approach to an accountant because you are talking language that he understands, and it opens the door.

In talking with a doctor, you can use this approach: "When people come to you, doctor, and they say that they are not well, what is the first thing you try to do? Diagnose their case? The second thing you do is to tell them what to do about it, don't you? Then you tell them how to do it, but you never make them do it. Doctor, this is what God does in His Word. He tells us what is wrong with us, He tells us what to do about it, and He tells us how to do it, but He never makes us do it. It is up to us to do it if we want to be made whole."

You may talk about riding in an automobile. Almost everybody in our day and time who is old enough has a driver's license and drives an automobile sometime. Talk to him about the red flashing lights and the clanging bells at railroad crossings. Ask what it means if one is approaching a railroad crossing and sees the flashing lights and hears the clanging bells. It means danger: a train is coming. And just so, God has put in His Word some red lights and some clanging bells that say *danger, danger ahead!* Would it not pay one to heed the danger signals? These are simple things, but they open the door for witnessing.

7.B.7. ASK THE PERSON HOW THEY WOULD GET TO HEAVEN

Other ways can be used to begin a witness. For instance, ask a leading question. In a casual conversation, say to the person, "Can you tell me how to get to heaven?" If he tells you the right way, ask him if he has taken that way. If he has not, ask if you may talk with him a few minutes about what the Bible says. If he tells you the wrong way, say to him, "The Bible says . . ." and go from there.

A rather catchy question which works well in areas like New Orleans with people of Catholic background is to say to the person, "Do you know if you are born once, you will die twice, but if you are born twice, you will just die once?" People who don't know anything about the new birth will ask what you mean. When they ask, turn to John 3 and tell them what you mean.

Again, one may ask the question, "Can you tell me how to be saved?" I had an interesting experience in 1957 when I went to the Orient to visit mission fields. In flying from Los Angeles to San Francisco, I was seated next to an Orthodox Jew and had the opportunity to witness to him. In a casual conversation, I asked him, "Can you tell me how to be saved?" He told me what he thought, then I asked him if I could tell him what I believed and why I believed it. I then took my New Testament and witnessed to him for the Lord.

On the plane from Honolulu to Tokyo I was seated next to a girl who knew nothing at all but Catholicism. She was from the Philippines, but she had been reared in a Catholic convent in Spain. She didn't know much about the Bible. I asked her if she could tell me how to be saved. When she told me what she believed about it, I asked her if I could tell her what I believed and why I believed it. I then took my New Testament and witnessed to her.

In Japan I was on a train from Fukuoka to Yahata. I went into the dining car but could not read the Japanese writing. A young Japanese man seated across the aisle from me saw that I was having trouble and asked if he could help me. I found out that he had spent about ten or twelve years in San Francisco, where his father was a Buddhist priest. I had the privilege of witnessing to him by asking him if he could tell me how to be saved. When he told me what he believed, I asked him if I could tell him what I believed, and I did witness to him. Not one of these was saved at that time, but not one of them had ever before heard the gospel.

In Hong Kong I went to a Hindu Temple and began to look around, as I had never been in a Hindu Temple before. One of the missionaries with me went over to witness to the priest. After she had witnessed, I asked the priest the question, "Can you tell me how to be saved?" He told me what the Hindus believe, and I then had the privilege of witnessing to him with the New Testament.

In Indonesia, flying from Bandung to Surabaya on a DC-3 airplane, I was seated next to an Indonesian businessman. He spoke good English, and I found out that he was a Muslim. I asked him the same question, "Can you tell me how to be saved?" After he told me what he believed, I took my New Testament and witnessed to him.

These five people were adherents of different religions, and the door was opened in every case by the simple question, "Can you tell me how to be saved?" If you ask a person, "Can you tell me how to be saved," and he tells you what he believes, out of courtesy he will listen to you. That is what we want, is it not? We are not commissioned to win them, we are commissioned to witness to them, and the Holy Spirit does the winning. He will win some if we are faithful in witnessing.

Whether a man accepts the Bible as God's Word or not, it is God's Word, and it is the Sword of the Spirit. So, plant the Sword of the Spirit in the man's heart so that the Spirit can use it. Even if he doesn't believe it, it is planted there, and the Spirit can use it. Many people have had doubts about the Bible, but there is no problem about the Scriptures when Jesus is Lord.

CHAPTER 8

THE SOUL-WINNER'S MESSAGE

8.A. PRESENTING THE PLAN OF SALVATION

We come now to discuss presenting the plan of salvation. How does one present the plan of salvation? How does one take the New Testament to show the person from the Scriptures that he is lost, that he needs to be saved, that he may be saved, and how to be saved? Whatever approach one makes, there comes a time when he says, "May I talk with you about this?" Then take the New Testament, open it to the first Scripture verse, and read it. Talk to the person about the meaning of this.

The first verse is Romans 3:10 (KJV): "As it is written, There is none righteous, no, not one." Ask the person something like this: "Have you ever known anyone who is perfect? No, there is no one perfect, and this is what this verse says: 'There is none righteous, not even one.'" When you ask a person, "Have you ever known anyone who is perfect," and he says no (and he most probably will), you can say, "That is what this verse says. This means that Gray Allison is not perfect, and this means that Joe Doakes (the person to whom I am talking) is not perfect." Get him to agree that he is not perfect. You see, no person ever goes to the doctor to be cured until first of all he knows that he is sick. So, nail it down!

Go to the second verse (Romans 3:23 KJV): "For all have sinned and come short of the glory of God." "Now, that word *all* is a small word, but it is a large word too, because it means that every person in the world is a sinner. This means Gray Allison is a sinner, this means that Joe Doakes is a sinner." It is good to include oneself, in the beginning especially. All of us have sinned. Do not assume that he knows what sin is. Many people do not know what sin is—they think only of murder, adultery, drunkenness, dope addiction, gambling, etc. as sin. They may not do any of these things, so talk to them about what this word *sin* means. The word *sin*, of course, carries the idea of "missing the mark," and one may say to him, "We have all missed the mark, we have failed to measure up to what God expects us to be. That is what the last part of the verse says: 'We have come short of the glory of God.'"

It is good to talk about sins that really come from our sin nature. For instance, say to the person, "Have you ever told a lie?" Well, is there anyone who has never told a lie? "Would you say that lying is a sin? What does God say? 'Thou shalt not bear false witness'" (Exodus 20:16 KJV). Now, if a person tells a lie, that is a sin against God, for he has broken the commandment of God. This person begins to realize then that he has sinned against God in that he has broken God's law. The devil is certainly shrewd. He doesn't mind us admitting sin in general. Have you ever noticed that people don't talk much about lying? They say, "I told a little fib, or a little white lie, or a story." You see, this is the devil's strategy. If he can get us to cover up this thing, he will. It does not sound nearly as bad to say, "I told a fib," as it does to say, "I lied." But lying is a sin against God.

Ask the person, "Have you ever stolen anything?" He probably will answer that he has never stolen anything. "Do you mean you have never eaten your sister's candy without asking her permission first? You never took an apple off of somebody's tree? That is stealing. Stealing is taking something that does not belong to you without permission. And stealing is a sin. God says, 'Thou shalt not steal'" (Exodus 20:15 KJV). We are trying to help a person to see that he has sinned against God.

Now, turn to the third verse. Say to him, "Yes, we have all sinned, and the Bible says sin does something to us. [Read Isaiah 59:2 KJV.] God said, 'But your iniquities have separated between you and your God, and your sins have hid his face from you, that he will not hear' (Isaiah 59:2 KJV). Your iniquities, your wrongdoings, have separated you from God. The idea of iniquity is the idea which is contained in our English word *wrong*. It means 'wrong,' 'warped,' or 'twisted.' Your twisted doings, your wrongdoings, your iniquities, have separated you and your God, and your sins have hidden His face from you."

Take a gospel tract (or something else) and put it between your fingers. Say to the person something like this: "This little gospel tract separates my fingers from each other. How can my fingers get together?" He will answer that they cannot get together until the tract is removed. So long as that paper is between those fingers, they can never get together. God says this is what sin does to us—it builds a wall between us and God. It separates us from God, and we can never get to God until that sin is removed. God is good to everybody. Didn't Jesus say, "He maketh his sun to rise on the evil and on the good, and sendeth rain on the just and the unjust?" (Matthew 5:45 KJV). God blesses everybody. But God's blessing on a person doesn't mean that the person is right with God! The Bible says that sin separates us from God, and we can never be right with God until that sin is removed.

Turn to Romans 6:23 and say, "The Bible also says in Romans 6:23 (KJV), 'The wages of sin is death.' Sin has a payday. One of these days sin is going to pay off, and it will pay off in death." Ask the person what he does for a living. Say, "When payday comes, you expect your wages, don't you? You have worked all the week, and on payday, you expect the wages promised you. Now, God said that sin has a payday, sin draws wages. The day is coming when sin will pay off, and the payday of sin is death. Is this talking about physical death? Yes, but more than that, spiritual death. Revelation 21:8 tells what the second death is. It is the lake that burns with fire and brimstone, Jesus said. Hell is the second death."

Using that tract between your fingers, say, "Joe, this is what that really means: A man sins and sins and sins in this life. His sin separates him from God. Now suppose he dies physically with that sin unforgiven, without that sin ever being taken away. He dies separated from God, and there is never any opportunity after physical death to have that sin taken away. Therefore, that sin separates him from God forever. That is the payday of sin—separation from God forever and forever. The worst thing about hell is that one is separated from God forever and forever." Now, you have shown him with these four verses of Scripture why he needs to be saved: he is a sinner and sin separates him from God and will keep him separated from God forever unless that sin is taken away. Now ask him, "Can you take away your own sin? Can you forgive your own sins, can you blot out your own sins? No, I can't forgive my sins, you can't forgive your sins. We need somebody to do something for us, don't we?"

Turn to John 3:16 and tell him that God has done something for us that we could not do for ourselves. Read to him John 3:16 (KJV): "For God so loved the world that he gave his only begotten Son, that whosoever believeth in him should not perish, but have everlasting life." Make that personal. Say to him, "Joe, if God loves the whole world, he loves Joe Doakes, doesn't he? *Whosoever* means what? Anybody! That means Gray Allison, and it means Joe Doakes. Joe, you can put your name in this verse of Scripture and not do damage to it at all. 'For God so loved Joe Doakes, that he gave his only begotten Son, that when Joe Doakes believes in him, he should not perish (not be separated from

God), but have everlasting life.' Joe, I can't explain that to you, because I do not understand it. The lights are burning, but I don't understand electricity."

I use a personal illustration here. "I was twelve years old when we got electricity at our house. We had gas lights and coal oil lamps until then. I didn't understand electricity when I was twelve years old, but I surely did enjoy it. The electric lights didn't flicker. We got a second-hand refrigerator and a Sears Roebuck radio. I enjoyed electricity, and still do, but I still don't understand it. If I had waited until I could understand it, I never would have enjoyed it! I don't understand how Jesus could die for your sins and my sins. I don't understand how the death of Jesus on the cross nineteen hundred years ago means that I do not have to be separated from God and you do not have to be separated from God. I do not understand how God can forgive sin through Jesus. But thank God, I do not have to understand it. I know what God says, and I know that God always tells the truth. When I was eleven years old, I believed God and trusted Him to do what He said He would do. Now I know the truth of it, though I still don't understand it. If we had to wait until we could understand electricity to enjoy it, we would never enjoy it. If we had to wait until we could understand salvation to enjoy it, we would never enjoy it. But we don't have to understand it."

Say to the person, "The real question is, how can you have this salvation? You know you need salvation; you have already told me so. God has provided salvation for you, but how can you get it? Let us see what God says." Turn to Acts 20:20-21 and tell him a little of the background. Paul was talking to the elders from Ephesus. He had preached there for about three years and had gone off on a missionary trip. He had returned to Miletus, near Ephesus. He called for the leaders of the churches of Ephesus to talk with him. When they came, he told them what he had preached to them while he was with them. He said, "And how I kept back nothing what was profitable unto you," (I didn't keep back anything you need to know) "but have shewed you, and have taught you publicly, and from house to house, Testifying both to the Jews, and also to the Greeks, repentance toward God, and faith toward our Lord Jesus Christ" (Acts 20:20-21 KJV). He told them everything they needed to know. He said it to the Jews and to the Greeks alike. That means that everybody in his day was told the same thing. Why? Because everybody has the same need. We are all sinners. Here is what Paul told them: "Repentance toward God, and faith toward our Lord Jesus Christ." Tell him what *repentance* and *faith* mean. Don't assume that he knows. Never assume that a person knows anything when you start to witness to him for Jesus. Talk to him as if he were a little child who didn't know very much about it, because most people do not know. Explain to him what repentance means and what faith means.

Repentance means to change one's mind. Repentance toward God means a person changes his mind toward God. A man sins and he sins and he sins. Every sin is against God. So every sin pushes him away from God, as if he were walking away. One day he says to himself, *This is not what I want. I don't want to move away from God, I want to be the person God wants me to be.* So he turns his life around, and instead of moving away from God, he moves toward God. The desire of his heart is to be the person God wants him to be. This is what repentance is. When a man knows that he has sinned against God, and he has a deep-seated desire not to be a sinner but to be the person God wants him to be—that is changing his mind toward God. This changes the direction of his life. This is repentance, but that is not enough to save him.

Say to him, "Joe, when I started talking to you, I asked if you knew anyone in the world who is perfect, and you said, 'No, nobody in the world is perfect.' Suppose you could start today and live an absolutely perfect life, turn away from sin and never sin again. What would you do with the sins that are back there in the past already? You can't do anything about them, can you? All the good you will ever do can never blot out the sins that are already committed. Joe, you need a Savior from sin, and this is why Paul said, 'Faith toward our Lord Jesus Christ.' You need someone who can take away the sins of the past, and you need someone who can give you power to live like God wants you to live right now and in the future. That is why the Apostle Paul said, 'Faith toward our Lord Jesus Christ.'

"Joe, let me illustrate what that word *faith* means. You had faith in that chair when you sat down. What is a chair for? A chair is to hold you off the floor. Now, Joe, when you sat on that chair, you believed it would do what it was supposed to do, and you trusted it to do it. So you committed your whole weight to that chair. Now, if you had not believed that chair would hold you up, you wouldn't have trusted your whole weight to the chair. You believed it would do what it is supposed to do, you trusted it to do it, you committed your weight to it. That is what faith is.

"To have faith toward our Lord Jesus Christ means that you believe Jesus will do what He says He will do, you trust Him to do it, you commit your whole life to Him. What did Jesus say He would do? Jesus said He will take away all of the sin that separates you from God. He said He will give you everlasting life. (That word *everlasting* means exactly what it says: it will last forever.) More than this, Jesus said He will give you the power of God in your life to help you every day to be the person God wants you to be. If you believe that Jesus will do what He says He will do, it is a matter of trusting Him to do it. This means to commit your whole life to Jesus Christ.

"Joe, you told me that you know you have sinned, and you know now what sin does because the Bible tells us. Let me ask you a few questions: In your heart, do you want to be the person God wants you to be? Do you really desire to turn from sin and be the person God wants you to be?" If he says yes, then say to him, "Joe, do you believe God will do what He says He will do?" If he says yes, do not leave it there.

Talk to him about what this decision for Christ means. One reason we have so many unregenerate church members is that they have never known really what it means to trust Jesus. To trust a chair means that you have committed your whole weight to it. Now, to trust Jesus means that you commit your whole life to Him. Acts 20:20-21 tells exactly what one must do: (1) One must repent. Jesus said, "I tell you, Nay, but, except ye repent, ye shall all likewise perish" (Luke 13:3 KJV); and (2) one must have faith in Jesus. John said, "This is His commandment, that we should believe on His son (have faith in His Son)," and Paul puts these together in this verse. Paul uses the word *Lord* before *Jesus Christ*.

To really accept Jesus to do what He said He will do means that one accepts Him as the Lord of his life. That word *Lord* means "boss" or "master." A boss is someone who tells you what to do, when to do it, where to do it, and how to do it. He is the boss. Say to him, "Joe, if someone is your boss and he tells you what to do, what are you supposed to do? Do it! All right, if you trust Jesus Christ to do what He said He will do, it means that you accept Him as the boss of your life from now on. He is the One to tell you what to do, where to do it, when to do it, and how to do it. He is your boss, and that means that from now on you take orders from Him, and you do what He wants you to do. Is this what you would like to do today? That means if Jesus Christ said, 'I want you to go to Nigeria and be a missionary, or to Korea and be a missionary, or to Alaska and be a missionary,' would you be willing to go?" When you see a person is not willing to go anywhere and do anything Jesus wants him to do, he has not committed his life to Jesus. Jesus is not his Lord. There must be a moment in a person's life when he has no reservation, no qualification at all, and he commits his life to the lordship of Jesus Christ. If every person who joined our churches would mean, "Yes, Jesus is my Lord, He is the boss of my life," we would have different churches. So lead the person to see it is the lordship of Jesus Christ. Jesus is nobody's Savior until first of all He is that person's Lord.

This concludes the presentation of the plan of salvation. Suppose when you come down to the close and ask him if he will do this, he says no, or he just doesn't say, use some of the closing verses. Turn to Revelation 3:20 and say something like this: "Joe, I came up to your house and I knocked on the door. You came to the door and invited me to come into your house. If you had not invited me in, I would have never entered your house. Never have I pushed my way into anyone's house. I have waited to be invited. Joe, Jesus stands and knocks. He said, 'Behold, I stand at the door, and knock: if any man hear my voice, and open the door, I will come in to him, and will sup with him [that means live with him], and he with me' [Revelation 3:20 KJV]. Joe, Jesus said He knocks at the door of your heart. He wants to come in, but He waits for you to open the door, to invite Him to come in. Will you today open your heart and invite Jesus Christ to come to be the Lord in your life? Jesus will never push His way into anybody's life, but He knocks and wants to come in. He waits for you to open the door. Joe, will you open the door of your heart and invite Jesus to come in to be your Lord?"

Now, if he doesn't say yes, but he is still receptive, move on to another verse. John 1:12 (KJV) is a good closing verse. "But as many as received Him, to them gave he power to become the Sons of God, even to them that believe on His name." Say, "Isn't that wonderful, Joe? God says in the Bible, 'As many as received Jesus into their hearts, as many as believe on His name, commit themselves to Him, to them God gives the power to become a Son of God.' You have told me that this is what you want—you want to be right with God. You want to be a child of God. God says the way to become right with Him, the way to be a child of God, is to receive Jesus Christ as Lord and Savior, to believe on Him. That means to trust Him to do what He said He would do. Will you do that today?"

If he doesn't say yes, turn to another passage, such as Romans 6:23. This is a good one to use again. Say to him, "Joe, we read a part of a verse a while ago. It says the wages of sin is death, but it also says, 'the gift of God is eternal life, through Jesus Christ our Lord.'" Use a gospel tract here and say to him, "Joe, this little tract I have been holding in my hand is a gift to remind you of my visit in your home. Would you take this?" Give it to him, then say to him, "Joe, is that your tract?" He will say, "Yes, it is mine." "When did it become yours? It became yours when you took it, didn't it? I meant it when I said, 'Joe, I want to give you this.' As far as I was concerned, I was giving it to you, but it did not become yours until you received it. Joe, God offers to you today the gift of eternal life. It is yours only if you take it. God has already paid for your salvation by the death of Christ. God has provided salvation. It is yours if you will receive it. How do you receive it? Paul tells us it is through Jesus Christ our Lord. If you will receive Jesus as the Lord of your life, you will receive God's gift of eternal life. Joe, will you receive that gift today?"

Perhaps he will say, "Well, I can't live up to it. I don't know if I can really do all that is involved." Say to him, "Well, Joe, that tract is yours, isn't it? It became yours when you took it. Suppose I said to you, 'Joe, give me a quarter and I will give you this tract.' Would that have been a gift to you? No. You would have been earning it. Joe, you can't earn a gift, and you can't pay for a gift. Now, God says that eternal life is the gift of God. You can't earn it, and you can't pay for it, or it wouldn't be a gift. The only way you will ever get it is to receive it as a gift. The only way you will ever get it is to receive Him as your Lord and Savior. Wouldn't you take God's gift of life today, by receiving His Son as your Lord?"

If the person begins to disagree, tactfully close the interview and leave him so you can come back again. Ask him if you may pray with him. Pray for him out loud, calling him by name, and ask God to convict him of his sins, ask God to point him to Jesus, and ask God to save him. Do not be embarrassed to pray for him. Specific prayer brings a specific answer; general prayer brings a general answer. After you have prayed for him, look up and say to him, "Joe, wouldn't you like to settle this thing today?" It gives you another opportunity without his feeling so much pressure. He knows that you are concerned, or you wouldn't have prayed for him.

If he says no, or he doesn't say, there is still one other opportunity to witness. Use the gospel tract. You have given it to him, so tell him, "Joe, I appreciate visiting in your home today. You have been gracious and kind, and I really appreciate talking with you. But I don't want to leave without showing you what I gave you." Take the tract back and show it to him. This gives the opportunity to go through the plan of salvation again. Ask him, "Joe, wouldn't you like to do that today?"

I asked a man seventeen times one Sunday afternoon if he would trust Jesus as his Lord. (I didn't count them, but the preacher with me did.) Sixteen times he said, "Not today." The seventeenth time, he said, "Not today—I will do it right now!" He didn't even take a breath between "today" and "I!" He was saved!

If the person to whom you are talking does not commit his life to Christ, say to him, "Joe, thank you for letting me talk with you. I really want you to have this tract. I gave it to you; it is yours. You don't have to have anyone here talking to you. After I am gone, get off somewhere by yourself and read through this tract. You can bow your heart before God and ask Jesus Christ to become your Lord and Savior. Will you read it after I am gone?" It is an easy thing to use a tract as an excuse not to witness, but tracts can be used to witness.

If, when you ask him to trust Christ, he says, "Yes, I would like to do this," then say, "Let us do what the Bible says. The Bible says confess with your mouth that Jesus is your Lord. Let us bow our heads. If you will, pray out loud and tell God that you know you have sinned and you need a Savior, and right now you are trusting Jesus Christ to be your Lord and Savior. Just invite Him into your heart as you invited me into your home a while ago." If he seems not to be able to pray out loud at all, ask him if he will let you pray and repeat after you. Pray the sinner's prayer for him and ask him to repeat after you. Try never to leave a man who says he has trusted Jesus until he has prayed by himself out loud. Nail it down! After he prays, tell him that is wonderful, and give him a verse or two of Scripture for assurance. Turn back to John 3:16 and talk about everlasting life, life that never ends.

Ask him if he has a Bible. If he has a Bible of his own, take his Bible and, in front of it on a blank page, write, "I trusted Jesus Christ as my Lord and Savior on October 23, 1964, when Brother Gray Allison talked with me. Signed . . . ." Ask him to sign his name. Under his signature, write John 3:16. Tell him again what it means. Then tell him if the devil ever comes to give him any doubts, turn and read what is written in his Bible and to read what God says in John 3:16. There is assurance!

Don't leave him until he has prayed out loud. Now praying out loud won't save a man, but it will nail this thing down for him. This is the time to teach him to pray out loud. Say to him, "Isn't it marvelous what God does for us? What do you do, Joe, when somebody gives you something? You say, 'thank you.' That is normal and natural as daylight following dark. Joe, today God has given you the most wonderful thing in the world, the greatest gift in the world—eternal life in Jesus! (See Romans 6:23.) Wouldn't you like to thank God for saving you today? Let's bow our heads again, and you just use your own words. Just thank Him for saving you today. Will you do that?"

8.B. DEALING WITH VARIOUS TYPES OF PEOPLE

How does one deal with different types of people? Do not try to answer all the questions and objections. Stay with the main thing—show them in the Word that they need to be saved, they may be saved, and how to be saved. Say to them, "Let's deal with some primary things first. Then I will be glad to stay as long as you want me to and try to answer any question you have. But let's look at these primary things first." Then show them the Scripture. If they push you on something, sometimes you may have to answer a question, but generally speaking, do not try to answer questions. Most of the time if you will use the Scriptures and talk to them about commitment to Jesus Christ, the questions will not arise. Many times, these questions are raised in order to avoid an issue.

8.B. 1. THE PERSON INTERESTED IN THE GOSPEL

Let us think first of all about dealing with the interested person. Many people in this world are genuinely interested in being saved but do not know the way to accept Christ. When one makes an approach to an interested person, they should present the plan of salvation as clearly and as simply as possible. Ask that this person make a commitment to Jesus Christ. If the person does not make the commitment to Christ, then try to find out the reason why. A good thing to do is to go back through the plan of salvation again.

Many times, a person does not understand something. If they are an adult, especially, they may hesitate to ask a question because they do not want to expose their ignorance of the Bible or the things of God. So many times this person, rather than ask a question to clarify something, will simply say, "No, I will not do that at this time, I will think about it." Therefore, go back through the plan of salvation and make it as plain as possible, then ask again for a commitment. If the person does not commit his life to Christ at this time, ask if they really are interested in salvation and desire to be saved. Try to find out why they will not make a commitment. Many times, it is something very simple and easy to deal with, if one can find out why they do not make the commitment to be saved.

8.B.2. DEALING WITH PEOPLE THAT THINK THEY ARE MORALLY GOOD

A second general classification into which many people fall is the so-called "good moral group." How does one deal with the person who claims to be living a clean moral life? The basic approach is always the same—that is, go through the plan of salvation in the Word of God and attempt to lead the person to a real commitment to Jesus Christ. If he then speaks of his own moral goodness and tells you that he does not need a Savior, I suggest the use of the scriptural illustrations of moral people who needed to be saved.

An excellent example is found in the tenth chapter of Mark's Gospel, verses 17-22 (NASB). The rich young ruler came to Jesus and said to him, "Good Teacher, what shall I do to inherit eternal life?" Jesus, you will remember, asked him a question: "Why do you call me good, there is none good, save one, that is God." I believe Jesus was saying to the young man, "Do you know to whom you are talking? Do you really understand that I am God? Is that why you addressed me as good?" And then Jesus told the young man something to do. He said, "Keep the commandments." The young man swelled his chest out in pride and said, "These things have I done from my youth up." But note carefully, Jesus began listing the commandments down toward the middle of the list. Jesus did not begin with the first commandment. Many people claim to be good morally but they say, "I believe all a person needs to do is to keep the Ten Commandments." If a person says this, agree with him, for if a person will keep the first commandment, really keep it, then the others will fall into their places, and a person is saved through the keeping of the first commandment. The yielding of one's heart, mind, soul, and all to God can be done only through

Jesus Christ. For Jesus said, "No man cometh unto the Father, but by me" (John 14:6 KJV).

Another scriptural illustration of a moral man who needed to be saved is Nicodemas. In the third chapter of John's Gospel, we find the record of Jesus dealing with Nicodemas. Nicodemas, evidently sincere, came to Jesus to talk with Him about salvation. Notice what the Bible says about this man. It speaks of him as a Pharisee. The Pharisees were the "good, moral" people of the day in which Jesus lived. They would not knowingly do anything wrong; they would not even pick up a stick on the sabbath day, and Nicodemas was a Pharisee. Note again that the Bible speaks of him as a ruler of the Jews—that is, he was a leader in the religious life of his day, and he was a master teacher of the Scriptures. Now Jesus said to this man, "Verily, verily, I say unto you, except a man be born again, he cannot see the Kingdom of God" (John 3:3 KJV). In verse 5 Jesus said, "Verily, verily, I say unto you, except a man be born of water and of the Spirit, he cannot enter into the Kingdom of God." Ask the person to whom you are talking, "Can you even measure up to the stature of Nicodemas? Can you say that you would not knowingly do anything wrong, that you are a religious leader of your day, and that you are a master teacher of the Scriptures?" Jesus said to this man who, measured by the world's standards and by man's standards, was a good man, "You cannot get into the kingdom of God unless you are born again." And then Jesus told him how to be born again. In verses 14 through 16 Jesus told him that the new birth comes as a person looks to Jesus Christ as his sin bearer and accepts Him as Savior. This is what John 3:16 says, that there is no other way of salvation.

Another good passage of Scripture with which to deal in talking to the "good, moral person" is the third chapter of Romans. There, Paul talks about our unrighteousness, our sin, our need of a Savior. He points to the complete righteousness of Jesus and tells us that the righteousness of Jesus may be imputed to us when we commit our hearts and lives to Him. Urge, then, this "good, moral person" to make the commitment of his life to the Lord Jesus that he may be made righteous by God's Son.

If this man does not respond by committing his life, go back to the plan of salvation and tell him again from God's Word that all of us have sinned and this includes him. Tell him again what sin does, tell him again what God has done for us, tell him again of this need of repentance and of commitment to Christ. Urge him to make this commitment to the Savior.

8.B.3. DEALING WITH SPIRITUALLY INDIFFERENT PEOPLE

How does one deal with the indifferent person? The prospect may be very cordial and may invite you into his home. He will listen to everything you have to say, and when you get through you are through. He sits there and lets you talk, and when you get through you are just through. Some people are completely or seemingly indifferent, as we go to witness to them for the Lord. Always, with every person, regardless of who he is or where he is from, deal with the plan of salvation. Go through the Scriptures that show him that he is a sinner and he needs to be saved, that he may be saved because Jesus loved him and died for him, and that he may be saved when he repents toward God and exercises faith toward our Lord Jesus Christ.

Ask him then if he will make this commitment to the Lord Jesus. This is basic! For a person who has been indifferent, this time go to him and give him the Word of God. The Holy Spirit uses the Word of God. He uses it during the interim between witnesses, and He will use it during the time you are witnessing again. Sometimes all one has to do with this man who is indifferent is to give him the Scripture and ask him to make this commitment.

You have dealt with him with the plan of salvation, and he is indifferent . . . how then do you try to bring him out of the indifference? Many ways can be used to help someone in their indifference, but one of the most effective is to ask him some questions. For example:

(1) "Can you go on being indifferent when you think about what Jesus did for you when He died on the cross?" Use Romans 5:8 (KJV), "God commendeth his love towards us in that while we were yet sinners, Christ died for us." Talk with him about the death of Christ. One of the most effective things in dealing with indifferent people is to tell them what Jesus did when He died on that cross.

Go back through the passion account in the Gospels and tell him of the death of Christ. Tell him of the last hours of Jesus on this earth and of the prayer of Jesus there in the garden: "Father if thou be willing, remove this cup from me: nevertheless not my will, but thine, be done" (Luke 22:42 KJV). Talk to the lost man about it. Was Jesus just shrinking from physical death? What cup was He talking about? He was talking about the cup of the wrath of God on sin. He was facing the cross. There was torment and suffering in the physical aspect of the cross. And, that was not the cup from which Jesus shrank. Tell the lost man of the cross. The cry of Jesus from the cross, "My God, my God why hast thou forsaken me?" (Luke 15:34 KJV) was not an idle cry. Jesus was not just a child of His times. Jesus was never less than God. Jesus did not just accommodate Himself to the times in which He lived. The Savior never one time spoke an idle word. The Savior was never mistaken. The penalty for sin is separation from God. Did Jesus pay the penalty for our sins? Yes, He paid the penalty for our sins on the cross. If all that He did was lay down His physical life and die on the cross, that is not enough.

A lot of people have died for their friends or given life to save the life of a friend, but Jesus Christ paid the penalty for our sins when He died on the cross. Tell this man that. Take him to the cross and talk to him about what Jesus did when He died on the cross. Say to him, "Can you go on being indifferent when you realize that Jesus Christ, God's Son, the Lord of Lords, the King of Kings, the heir of the glories of heaven, came into this world and took on Himself the form of a servant, became obedient unto death, even the death on the cross? He died on that cross for your sins and my sins." Make a personal application; tell him what his sin is going to bring, that the penalty of sin is separation from God, and that Jesus paid that penalty. He may have salvation from sin, from Satan, and from self—all that is involved in salvation; but he must make a life commitment to Jesus Christ. If he can remain indifferent when he hears the story of the cross, his heart is indeed hardened. Few people can remain indifferent when they hear the story of the Lord Jesus. They may get embarrassed, they may get belligerent and want you to leave, but there are not many people who can remain indifferent when you tell them the story of the cross.

(2) If he is still indifferent, ask, "Can you go on being indifferent when you realize that your immortal soul is at stake? Jesus said, 'What shall it profit a man, if he shall gain the whole world, and lose his own soul? Or what shall a man give in exchange for his soul?' (Mark 8:36-37 KJV). Can you go on being indifferent when you realize we are not just dealing with your lifetime; we are dealing with your eternity?"

(3) A third question you might use if he is still indifferent: "Can you go on being indifferent when you realize that life is so uncertain?" If a man can be so frightened that he is not indifferent and unconcerned anymore, well and good. We need to remember that the Holy Spirit has to convict and convert. But the Holy Spirit uses human instrumentality to present the need to a man for the Spirit to bring conviction, and He shows that the need can be met—and the Holy Spirit shows a man how to meet this need. Talk to him about the uncertainty of life. Life is uncertain.

I sometimes ask the person how old a man has to be to die. That sounds silly, but it is surprising how many people say, "Oh, seventy-five or eighty." Ask, "Have you ever walked through a cemetery and noticed the ages recorded on the tombstones? Some babies are buried there, some children, some young men and women, middle-aged people, and old folks. Pick up your paper any day and read about somebody who died at a younger age than you. Some of them died a natural death, some died an accidental death—but they died. Life is uncertain." This is the thing he must see. He may not believe Jesus is coming again, but he knows that people die. Now, just being afraid to die will not save anybody, but if one is afraid he will die and go to hell, it will make him stop and think.

Salvation is much more than being saved from hell, but this is a part of it and may help a man to see the need of salvation.

Use the Scripture: Proverbs 27:1 (KJV) says, "Boast not thyself of tomorrow; for thou knowest not what a day may bring forth." Ask the person, "Can you guarantee me you will be alive at this time tomorrow?" Take a piece of paper and write on it: "I will not commit my heart and life to the Lord Jesus Christ for twenty-four hours under any condition." Ask, "Will you sign this?" If he says no, ask, "Why not?" Perhaps he will start to think about it—why not sign that? Because life is uncertain! The devil blinds a man's heart and mind, and the Word just doesn't get through, until somehow he stops to think about the matter. The devil conditions people, and over a period of time, a man could sit there and listen to you say all that you say but never really hear what you are saying. That man needs to stop and think for himself. If he will think about it, he will not remain indifferent. Luke 12:19 (KJV) is a good verse to use. Tell him about the man who said, "Soul . . . , take thine ease, eat, drink and be merry." God said to him, "Thou fool [why was he a fool? He had no concern for God; he was concerned only about the things of this world], this night thy soul shall be required of thee: then whose shall those things be, which thou hast provided?" (Luke 12:20 KJV).

(4) Another good question to ask the indifferent person is, "Can you go on being indifferent when you know who it is who stands and knocks at your heart? Do you realize that Jesus Christ is knocking at your heart and wants to come in?" Use Revelation 3:20 (KJV) and tell him who it is who wants to come into his life. "Behold, I stand at the door and knock: If any man hear my voice, and open the door, I will come in to him, and will sup with him, and he with me." Talk to him about what Jesus can do for his life. Tell him he may be saved from hell, but that is just part of it. He may be saved for service here in this life. Talk to him about the joy and glory and the happiness of serving God in this world. Isn't it a marvelous thing God has done for us to let us serve Him? Isn't it a marvelous thing that we may be partners with the Holy Spirit in the work of Christ? Hebrews 6:4 speaks of "partakers of the Holy Ghost." The word *partakers* is the word for "partners." We are partners with the Holy Spirit. Talk to him about the privilege of being a partner with the Holy Spirit of God in the work of God in this world. The greatest thing in the world is to have the privilege of serving God.

Ask him who are the happiest people he knows. Ask him who are the best people he knows. He will always tell you about the hypocrites in the church, but ask him who are the best people he knows and 999 times out of one thousand he is going to tell you about Christian people. Tell this man what he is missing by not letting Jesus come into his life. What is Jesus going to do for him? The best things! We give people the impression that it is an awfully hard thing to do the will of God. They are afraid to turn their lives over to Him because He may give them a bitter cup to drink. God does not do that. Did not Jesus say, "If ye then, being evil, know how to give good gifts unto you children, how much more shall your Father which is in heaven give good things to them that ask him?" (Matthew 7:11 KJV). How much more would He give good things! He doesn't want to do the bad things for us; He wants the good things for us. God knows better than we do. Tell this man that he is missing life without the Savior. Ask him, "Can you go on being indifferent when you realize that the Son of God wants to come into your life and make life what it ought to be?" Life with Jesus is life at its best; it is the only life. Tell him about the wonderful life with Jesus and it may bring him out of his indifference.

(5) Some people advocate the shock treatment. If you cannot make a man stop and think any other way, perhaps you may shock him into it. What does one think about when he gets angry? What happens when a man begins to think about the Lord and the people of the Lord? The Holy Spirit begins to work on him. Love and tactfulness are ways to win, but there are times when a man needs to be shocked out of his indifference. It is better to have a fellow angry at you and innerved by what you said than to have several pleasant conversations with him and have him maintain his indifference. Maybe doing something different will shock him out of his indifference!

8.B.4. DEALING WITH THE PERSON WHO WANTS TO DELAY A DECISION

How does one deal with a procrastinator? Basically, you deal with him as you do an indifferent person, because he is an indifferent person. He is the man who says, "I know I ought to do this; I believe everything you say. You are exactly right, this is what I need, and I am going to do that one of these days." He is hard to deal with because he agrees with everything you say. He is just indifferent! He is calloused and hard. This is his defense, and it is a good one. One goes away feeling so good because he witnessed to the man, and he is going to trust Christ one of these days.

An eighty-three-year-old man in Georgia was as kind and nice as could be when witnessed to. He said, "Preacher, I agree with everything you said. I know that is what I ought to do, and one of these days I am going to do it." Eighty-three-and-one-half years old! The witness said to him, "Sir, are you going to live to be a hundred years of age?" He said, "Not the way I feel today." "Are you going to live to be eighty-four?" He said, "I don't know, I may not live until tomorrow." The witness then said, "Well, if you are going to do this one of these days, then today is the today to do it." He said, "I believe it is," and he did. Now what had the devil done to him for eighty-three-and-one-half years? He hadn't said to him, "Don't you do it." The devil never says this. He just says, "Put it off, do it 'one of these days.'"

Show the procrastinator the danger of delay. Turn to James 4:13-14 (KJV), and read to him, "Go to now, ye that say, today or tomorrow we will go into such a city, and continue there for a year, and buy and sell, and get gain: Whereas ye know not what shall be on the morrow. For what is your life? It is even a vapour, that appeareth for a little time, and then vanisheth away." Use Proverbs 27:1 (KJV): "Boast not thyself of tomorrow, for thou knowest not what a day may bring forth." Proverbs 29:1 (KJV) is good here: "He, that being often reproved hardeneth his neck, shall suddenly be destroyed, and that without remedy."

Let us review some things. Always use the Scripture to show the person his need, the provision to meet the need, and how he may be saved. Never assume that he understands these things. Attempt to find out why he does not commit his life to Christ, and then show him Scripture that will help him.

8.B.5. DEALING WITH WORLD RELIGIONS AND MEMBERS OF CULTS

One deals with Roman Catholicism, Judaism, members of the Mormon cult, etc., as with other people. First, determine their relationship to Christ. Present the claims of Christ from the Scriptures on their lives. It is always good to know as much as possible about the prospect and his beliefs, but the basic thing to remember is to use the Word of God to show him his need of salvation, that he may be saved, and how to be saved.

A good approach to witness to any cult member is to state to them, "You can have five minutes to tell me how to get to heaven, and I will not answer any questions; just tell me how." Then say, "After you are done, then I will take five minutes and tell you what the Bible says is the true way to heaven." Since many cult members spend time studying how to ask you questions, this approach will be different for them. It also keeps you from getting into an argument or from feeling on the defensive if they ask you a question for which you do not have an answer.

8.C. FOLLOW UP: SIX ESSENTIAL MATTERS

If the person prays to receive Christ as their Savior, there are several things you should tell them. These are important matters for every believer, not just for someone who recently prayed to receive Christ. After the person prays and thanks God for saving him, don't leave him just there. Talk to him about the fact that he needs to be obedient to Christ. Ask him, "Jim, don't you really love Jesus Christ? You have confessed him as your Lord; that means that you love Him, doesn't it?" He will say yes. Read to him John 14:15. Jesus said, "If you love me, keep my commandments" (John 14:15 KJV). "Jim, I always ask a person to do six things when he gives his life to Christ. The first three of these go together, but I have separated them so that we may talk about them. The first is to profess Christ publicly. Jesus said in Matthew 10:32 (KJV), 'Whosoever therefore will confess me before men him will I confess before my Father in Heaven.' Will you come to the church and make a public profession of your faith to let people know that you love Jesus and that you have committed your life to Him?"

When he says yes, then say, "The second thing you need to do is to follow Christ in baptism. When Peter was asked on the Day of Pentecost what these men should do, he said, 'Repent, and be baptized, every one of you in the name of Jesus Christ' (Acts 2:38 KJV). And in Acts 2:41 the Scripture says, 'Then they that gladly received his word were baptized' (Acts 2:41 KJV)."

Now, this person doesn't understand what baptism is, so explain to him that baptism is a picture. It pictures the death of Christ for our sins, the burial of Christ, and His resurrection from the dead. Baptism also pictures, according to Romans 6, what happens to the person who trusts Christ as Lord. Paul says that the old man of sin has died, is buried with Christ, is gone forever, and is raised up a new person in Christ. Now, this makes baptism make sense to him. He needs to be immersed to show the picture of death, burial, and resurrection.

"The third thing, Jim, is to join a New Testament church. In Acts 2:47 (KJV) the Bible says, 'And the Lord added to the church daily such as should be saved.'" Now, why does he need to join the church? Many people think the church is a building. Some people think it is an organization. Help him to understand the nature and purpose of the church, and he will see his need for joining the church. Just say to him something like this: "Jim, you know the church is not a building, and it is not an organization. It is a home for God's children. A church is a place where God's people are gathered together—where they help one another and where they worship and praise and serve God." I use my children as an illustration. I say, "You know, when my daughter, Suzanne, was born on a cold, cold February day in 1949, I would have been a silly father to put her out in the yard at the hospital and say, 'Suzanne, we are so glad you were born; we love you so much, we wanted a little baby, honey,' and then say to her, 'The world is cold and cruel and hard, but I certainly hope you grow up to be a big, strong girl. God bless you now.' Now isn't that silly? She couldn't do it. A baby needs a home where people love her, help her, and teach her. Now that's what the church is, Jim, a home for God's children."

"Today you are thirty years old, physically and mentally, but you are a child in Christ. You have just been born into His family, and you need a home where people love you, help you, and teach you. That's what the church is. More than that, a home is a place a person has the opportunity to help others, and that's what the church is. It's a place where, as you learn and grow in Christ, you have an opportunity to help other people. Will you come and publicly profess Christ and ask for baptism and join a New Testament church?"

When he says yes, say, "I want to ask you a fourth thing. You told me that you have a Bible. Will you read God's Word daily? Jesus said in John 5:39 (KJV), 'Search the Scriptures..., they are they which testify of Me.'" Now, if you ask him to read the Bible and he agrees, the chances are that he will start with Genesis. He will read until he gets to the genealogical section of the Bible, the "begats," and he will never read again. He will not understand all of the names and why they are in the Bible. Do not let him do that. Ask him if he will begin to read John's Gospel. It is an easy-to-understand book. Read a chapter a day in the Gospel according to John. The Gospel of John tells him about Jesus' life and ministry. It will tell him about his own experience with Christ, so say this to him: "Jim, will you read a chapter every day in the Word of God?" If he says yes, ask him to do the fifth thing.

"Jim, will you pray every day? It says in Matthew 6:9 (KJV), 'Pray ye.'" Now he may not understand what prayer is. Tell him that we need to pray to God. Tell him that prayer is just talking to God—just like you would talk with a friend. Ask him to pray every morning when he first awakes and to thank God for saving him. This will give him assurance at the beginning of every day. Tell him also to pray to God and ask that God will help him to live that day like God wants him to live. You see, our tendency is to say, "Lord, help me to be a good Christian all my life." But we don't live life like that. We live it one day at a time. Ask him to pray to God that He will help him to live that day as he ought to live. Then ask him to confess his sin when he does sin. God's Holy Spirit convicts the child of God of sin. Then tell him, "When you do sin, immediately confess it and ask God's forgiveness, and ask Him to help you not to do it again."

A sixth thing to ask him to do is this: "Jim, will you witness for Christ every day? Jesus said in Luke 24:48, 'Ye are witnesses of these things.' Tell somebody every day what God has done for you; tell somebody every day of God's love for them. Speak to them about Christ." I ask him to do a special thing; I say, "Jim, will you tell the first person you see after we quit talking that you have asked Jesus Christ to come into your life, to be the Lord of your life?" This will nail down his experience; it gives him assurance. It will be a blessing in his life, and it will help him be a witness for Christ. This is the time to help him get involved in a church, to be a reader of the Word of God, to be a person of prayer, and to be a witness for Christ. You will have him started on a good Christian life of growth if you will do these things.

CHAPTER 9

THE IMPORTANCE OF EVANGELIZING ONE PERSON AT A TIME

The following article is from the *Royal Service Magazine* of the Woman's Missionary Union of the Southern Baptist Convention, Vol. 60, Number 7, January 1966, under the title "Person to Person." At that time, Dr. B. Gray Allison was the professor of missions at the New Orleans Baptist Theological Seminary. The original article incorrectly listed his name as "Gray B. Allison." The article follows in its entirety.

Often in the Gospel record of the life and labors of our Lord we find him bearing witness to individuals. How easy it is in our day to look at people, to preach to people, to think in terms of people. Perhaps we need instead to look at a person, to witness to a person, to think in terms of a person. We need to come out of the abstract into the particular and see people as individuals.

A poet imagined the Apostle Paul saying, "Only as souls I see the people." Oh, that we might see them like that! We do not find it difficult to go through the motions of religious activity. We joyfully participate in missionary reading "round tables," weeks of prayer for missions, special offerings to meet special needs. But when it comes to translating concern into daily, person-to-person witness for Christ, most of us no doubt would feel ourselves miserable failures. I have attended many WMU [Editor's Note: Woman's Missionary Union of the Southern Baptist Convention] meetings which thrilled my heart, but the thrill soon left as I realized that these women were talking about missions and praying about missions, but most of them were not "doing" missions. How can this be changed?

There are three words which furnish us the key—Lost, Lord, and Love. We must believe people are lost, we must acknowledge Christ as Lord, and we must love. My beloved professor, Dr. Roland Leavell, put it like this: How much do I care? How much of Christ do I have to share? How far will I dare?

We must believe that people without Christ are lost. Until the lostness of people is real to us, we will never really try to bring them to Christ so they can be saved. The Bible is filled with passages describing the lost condition of those who have not Christ. Paul said, "But if our gospel be hid, it is hid to them that are lost" (2 Corinthians 4:3 KJV). To be lost means that one has missed the way, he does not know the way home. Jesus said, "I am the way . . . no man cometh unto the Father, but by me" (John 14:6 KJV). John said, "Whosoever denieth the Son, the same hath not the Father" (1 John 2:23 KJV). How plain could the Bible make it? People have missed the way—the only way—to God, and are lost!

We must understand something of what it means to be lost. To be lost means there is a lack of peace in the life. "The wicked flee when no man pursueth" (Proverbs 28:1 KJV). "But the wicked are like the troubled sea, when it cannot rest" (Isaiah 57:20 KJV). To be lost means loss of the Presence, in other words, the loss of real life, for when one is not related to God, he has no life—he is separated from life (see Ezekiel 18:4; Romans 6:23; James 1:15). To be lost means lasting punishment. Hell awaits at the end of a Christless life (see Matthew 25:41, 46; Mark 9:43-48; 2 Thessalonians 1:7-9). A realization that our friends who are without Christ are lost, and a realization of what it means to be lost, will give us an imperative to win them for Christ.

General William Booth of the Salvation Army once said he would like to send all his candidates for officer positions to Hell for twenty-four hours. He felt that this would be the chief part of their training and would make them able to reach the lost.

We must unreservedly accept Jesus Christ as Lord. This will do many things. It will make us diligent students of the Word of God. It will make us people of prayer. The combination of these two things will help us grow in Christlikeness. The more we become like him, the greater will be our burden for the lost ones around us, for Jesus came "to seek and to save that which was lost" (Luke 19:10 KJV). He came "to call . . . sinners to repentance" (Matthew 9:13 KJV). When we unreservedly accept Jesus as Lord, it will compel us to go as witnesses for he has commanded it. Oh, can we not hear his words: "Why call ye me Lord, Lord, and do not the things which I say?" If he is Lord, we must witness for him. There can be no holding back.

We must love. The most compelling force in the world is love. Victor Hugo said, "The greatest happiness of life is the conviction that we are loved, loved for ourselves, or rather loved in spite of ourselves." Preaching may fail, singing may fail, but individual concern does not fail. I saw a hardened sinner come to Christ because a man named Vince Sparks cared for him and wept over him because of his heart-concern. J. H. Lowett said, "We cannot heal the wounds we do not feel."

Down in the human heart, Crush'd by the tempter,
Feelings lie buried that grace can restore;
Touch'd by a loving heart, waken'd by kindness,
Chords that are broken will vibrate once more.
—Fanny J. Crosby

It was a heart of love that made Jesus weep over a city. It was a heart of love that made Paul plead earnestly with sinners "night and day with tears." Peter urged, "Above all things be fervent in love."

The German philosopher Heine stood once, disillusioned and in despair, before the statue of Venus de Milo. He said, "Ah, yes! I suppose you would help me if you could, but you can't. Your lips are still and your heart is cold." May it not be that our lips are still because our hearts are cold!

Would you care if some friend you had met day by day
Should never be told about Jesus?

109

Would you care if she in the judgment should say
No one ever told me of Jesus?
—Carrie E. Beck and Charles H. Gabriel[34]

The real question is: How can I love sinners? The answer is: Fall in love with Jesus! A real love for Him will result in a real love for them! May God help us as we meet people in a doorway, in a supermarket, in a home, to be so in love with Jesus that we will cry with Jeremiah of old: "If I say, 'I will not mention him, or speak any more in his name,' there is in my heart as it were a burning fire shut up in my bones, and I am weary with holding it in, and I cannot" (Jeremiah 20:9, RSV). For you see,

He is counting on you,
On a love that will share
In His burden of prayer
For those he has brought
With His lifeblood, and sought
Through His sorrow and pain
To win home again.
He is counting on you—If we fail Him,
What then?
—Author Unknown[35]

CHAPTER 10

THE COMPLETE EVANGELISM OUTLINE

Most evangelistic materials follow a basic and logical model. This model can be replicated by anyone who produces their own tracts or other materials. The model included here incorporates the outline from Gray Allison's evangelistic materials.

10.A. THE PLAN OF SALVATION

(1) Introduction

(2) Transitional Questions
 2.1. Do you ever think about spiritual things?
 2.2. May I ask you a spiritual question?
 2.3. Have you come to the place in your own life where you know that if you died tonight you would go to heaven?
 2.4. Suppose you were to die tonight and stand before God, and He said, "Why should I let you into my heaven?" What would you tell Him?

(3) Salvation Needed
 3.1. The Fact of Sin
  3.1.A. Romans 3:10, "Ever know anyone who is perfect?"
  3.1.B. Romans 3:23, "You can put your name here . . . ."

3.2. The Consequences of Sin
    3.2.A. Isaiah 59:2, "The separation that sin brings"
    3.2.B. Romans 6:23, "What are wages?"

(4) Salvation Provided
    4.1. The Person and Work of Jesus Christ
        4.1.A. John 3:16

(5) Salvation Accepted
    5.1. Repentance Required
        5.1.A. Acts 20:20-21, "A change of mind"
    5.2. Faith is Necessary
        5.2.A. Acts 20:20-21, "Trusting in Christ alone for salvation"

(6) Invitation to Accept Christ
    6.1. Romans 10:13, "To call upon the name of the Lord"
    6.2. Call for a decision: "Does all of this make sense to you? Would you like to give your life to Jesus and ask Him to be your personal Lord and Savior?"
    6.3. Pray the sinner's prayer.

(7) First Steps in Following Jesus as Lord and Savior
    7.1. Closing verses: Revelation 3:20; Romans 10:9-13; Romans 6:23; John 1:12
    7.2. Public confession of faith: Matthew 10:32-33
    7.3. Believer's baptism: Matthew 28:18-20
    7.4. Church membership: Matthew 28:18-20; Acts 2:41, 47
    7.5. Read God's Word daily
    7.6. Pray every day
    7.7. Witness for Christ every day

10.B. AN EVANGELISM PRESENTATION MODEL

Beginning with this presentation, a model for evaluating evangelism materials may be developed. Most materials will follow a basic outline. Once one understands the outline, a local church could even develop its own evangelism materials. The advantage of this approach would be that the materials could be directly customized for the context and culture of their city or target audience.

10.B.1. PART ONE: THE INTRODUCTION

Almost anything can be used to begin a conversation that will result in a gospel presentation. Even a simple, "How are you today?" can result in a deeper conversation that will result in an opening for the gospel. People new to witnessing may need more direction here, but experienced witnesses can turn almost any conversation into a witnessing encounter.

10.B.2. PART TWO: THE TRANSITION

When a conversation or meeting has begun, the person doing the witnessing will almost always need to turn the conversation in a spiritual direction. If this is your initial encounter with a lost person, you may need to use a transitional question to make the conversation a spiritual one. On rare occasions the lost person may state their need for spiritual direction and then the witness can proceed. A series of diagnostic or transitional questions is included in the early part of this chapter. Remember, the best transitional questions cannot be answered with a "yes" or a "no." The question is intended to keep the dialogue going so that the plan of salvation may be presented.

10.B.3. PART THREE: SALVATION NEEDED

While a three-point outline is not a requirement to hear the gospel of Jesus Christ, the message of salvation should be presented in clear detail. Sin, repentance, and salvation should be discussed with a strong reliance on Scripture to make the points needed. The gospel plan outlined in the first part of this chapter can serve as an example for a comprehensive gospel presentation. Remember that each point is a biblical essential. The sinner must turn from sin and follow Jesus Christ as Lord and Savior.

Clearly establish that all people are sinners. Make sure that the person hearing the gospel understands that they, too, are a sinner. Without an admission of sin, there can be no real repentance from sin.

10.B.4. PART FOUR: SALVATION PROVIDED

John 3:16-17 gives very clear explanations of the provision of salvation for sinners. Emphasize the fact that salvation comes exclusively through Jesus Christ. State that the work of Jesus Christ on the cross and in the resurrection are enough to make a sinner right with God.

10.B.5. PART FIVE: SALVATION ACCEPTED

Make a decision for Christ as personal as you can. The Lord Jesus came specifically to save the soul of the person to whom you are talking. Also emphasize that they must make a personal decision to accept Christ as their Savior.

10.B.6. PART SIX: THE INVITATION TO ACCEPT CHRIST

This section details number six of the model plan of evangelism. As has been shown in the preceding chapters of this book, giving an invitation to an individual to accept Christ at the moment of the presentation of the gospel is biblical and necessary. Ask them, "Would you like to accept Jesus Christ as your personal Lord and Savior right now?" If they say yes, you can proceed to the sinner's prayer. If they say no, you can counsel them and work to make an opportunity to share the gospel with them again in the future. Much discernment is required here. Knowing when to end the witnessing encounter and when to push ahead requires a true reliance on the work of the Holy Spirit. Too often, the person doing the witnessing will quit too soon rather than push too hard. Remember, the person hearing the gospel is lost and is as far away from the Lord as they can be. You cannot drive them farther away from God, although you can make it more difficult for you to speak with them in the future.

I always encourage the person to pray on their own, but if they need assistance, you can lead them in a prayer of repentance and faith. Remind them that the words must be what they believe and desire to do in this moment. The following is a sample sinner's prayer:

> *Dear Lord, I know that I am a sinner. I know that I have done wrong. Forgive me of my sins. I believe in You, Jesus. I believe You died on the cross and rose from the dead for me. Come into my life and be my personal Lord and Savior. Thank You for saving me, Lord Jesus.*

10.B.7. PART SEVEN: FIRST STEPS IN FOLLOWING JESUS AS LORD AND SAVIOR

As the person leading someone to the Lord, you have a responsibility to help them in their first steps with Jesus Christ. They may not remember everything you say at that moment, but you need to share with them about believer's baptism and church membership. You should also make sure they know how to pray to the Lord and how to hear from God through reading His Word, the Bible. Being a member of a local, New Testament church is an essential part of their Christian journey. Baptist statesman Joe T. Odle wrote in his *Church Member's Handbook,*

> The church of the Lord Jesus Christ is the greatest institution that the world has ever known. Christ established it during his personal ministry, and he is its head (Matt. 16:18; Eph. 5:23; Col. 1:18). He promised that he would be with it through the ages and that the gates of hell should not prevail against it (Matt. 16:18; 28:20). To it he gave the Great Commission and the ordinances, and for it he

went to the cross (Matt. 28:19-20; 1 Cor. 11:23-26; Eph. 5:25). He loved the church, and he wants his churches to honor and glorify him as his representatives on the earth (Eph. 3:21; 5:25-27).[36]

10.C. EVALUATING EVANGELISTIC MATERIALS

While many methods of evangelism exist, only a few methods will be considered here. These methods will serve to show how evangelistic materials can be evaluated for use. These methods also remind us that we should prepare new believers to witness immediately and not give them the impression that evangelism is only for highly trained people.

10.C.1. USING GOSPEL TRACTS

A gospel tract is a small handout or brochure that can be given to a person in need of hearing the gospel. The tract can be used when time is short or if it is inconvenient to talk with a prospect at the moment you are with them. A tract is considered an easy level (Level 1) evangelism strategy and requires little or no training to be used in witnessing.

A good tract should, first and foremost, contain verses of Scripture, not just Scripture references. The tract should also clearly outline the gospel message and give a clear path to accepting Jesus Christ as Lord and Savior. A good question to ask is, if that tract was the only information that a lost person had with them, could they trust Christ based on the information in that tract? You can use the evangelism presentation model above to evaluate the value of the tract that is being used for evangelism. How many of the parts of the model does the tract include? What parts of the model are missing from the tract?

A good tract should be visually attractive to the target audience and should not look like a user's guide for complicated machinery. If the tract has both a verbal and visual plan of salvation, that is a definite positive aspect. Some type of contact information should be included on the tract for follow up. This could include a link to the church website with information on coming to Christ or an email address for further contact.

One excellent tract that has been used for years is the Four Spiritual Laws written by Bill Bright.[37] The gospel presentation in the tract is thorough and built around four main points: Law 1 states the love of God for the sinner and the plan that He has for the sinner's life; Law 2 discusses the sin nature of people and the consequences of that sin; Law 3 presents Jesus Christ as the answer for sin; and Law 4 shows that a sinner must accept Christ as personal Lord and Savior.

The strengths of this tract are that it has a full presentation of the gospel and includes the Scripture verses and not just the references. A person can witness to someone simply by reading the tract with them. The tract even includes follow-up instructions for a new believer and website addresses so that the new believer can find additional information on the Christian life.

Though some of the language may be somewhat dated and the illustrations require explaining, this tract has been effectively used for a number of years and continues to be an excellent tool for evangelism.

10.C.2. USING TESTIMONY-BASED EVANGELISM PRESENTATIONS

An intermediate level (Level 2) approach to witnessing is building a gospel presentation around a person's Christian testimony. Since the witness is sharing their own story, they can easily remember what to say. Scripture references should be learned to share along with the person's story. Though some marketed materials can be found, this approach is easy for a church to customize.

Most testimony-based approaches divide the story into three parts: (1) My life before Christ; (2) how I met Christ; and (3) my life after Christ. Using the evangelism presentation model, you can make an entire gospel plan while using the testimony as a means to share the gospel. Remember not to spend too much time talking about past sins, but focus on how you came to Christ and how the person hearing the story can make the same decision that you made. Make the gospel of Jesus the emphasis of the story.

The advantages of this approach are that a person can be quickly trained to begin witnessing. Also, since it is their story, they can avoid debates on distracting topics and other issues that may be related more to apologetics than just gospel witnessing. Eventually a person using this method should move up to a more detailed approach in order to give a stronger witness for Christ.

Web-based evangelism programs can also be used for the presentation of the gospel and for training witnesses. An example of web-based evangelism is *e3 Partners: Equip, Evangelize, Establish*. Their approach is entitled the Four Fields Method, and their mission is: equipping God's people; evangelizing His world; establishing His church. The Four Fields of Jesus' strategy are: entry, gospel, discipleship, and church.[38]

One of the most complete evangelism presentations is from Evangelism Explosion International Ministries.[39] This detailed presentation is a great resource and is a Level 3 program. It requires a high level of commitment and memorization of Scripture. It does take some time to complete the gospel presentation which could be a concern in certain settings.

Churches should provide several levels of evangelism training for members. Level 1 training could include using tracts or even a testimony-based evangelism program. Level 2 training could include materials that require some level of memorization of Scripture and an evangelistic outline. Level 3 training could include an approach like Evangelism Explosion which requires significant time commitment and learning a detailed approach to evangelism. No one approach works for every believer, and as believers gain experience and confidence in their evangelistic efforts, they may want to move from Level 1 to 2 to 3 as they witness.

CHAPTER 11

ISSUES IN EVANGELISM

P ortions of this article by B. Gray Allison originally appeared as "Issues In Evangelism" in the 1998 edition of the *Mid-America Baptist Theological Journal* vol. 22, pp 39–54. All Scripture references are from the KJV unless otherwise noted.[40]

This article concerns "Issues in Evangelism." However, space does not allow me to deal with a number of issues, so I have limited the scope of the article. In this day of a shrinking world, Christians are faced with many varying theological views. I wish to deal with several of these which I believe are dangerous and which tend to cut the nerve of evangelism. I have quoted more than usual, because the proponents of these (I believe) errant views clearly state their views.

11.A. UNIVERSALISM

Universalists believe that all people eventually will be saved. I suppose that all of us would like to think that. We would like to think that nobody will spend eternity in hell. It is amazing how many people *do* believe this.

The concept of universalism goes back at least as far as Origen of Alexandria (AD 185–254). Albert Henry Newman said that

Origen "Had a firm belief in the final restoration of harmony in the spiritual world. Even the damned and devils…would after having undergone sufficient disciplinary punishment, be brought into voluntary subjection to Christ" (1904, 285-86). The first universalist congregation was founded in the United States in Gloucester, Massachusetts, in 1779. Universalists merged with unitarians in the United States in 1960, but there are only about 200,000 members.

The danger to evangelism is not from the Unitarian-Universalist Association. The danger from universalism comes because the idea is held by many people in the mainstream of evangelical Christianity. D. T. Niles, a leader in the World Council of Churches in the second half of the twentieth century said:

The New Testament does not allow us to say either, 'yes' or 'no' to the question: "Will all men be saved?" And by preventing us from doing this it forces on us the question, "Will you fulfill your share of the task to which God has called you in the church – the task of making Jesus known and loved, confessed and obeyed, by all men in every area of life?" [1962, 96].

On page 97 Niles said, "It is that one must not succumb to the temptation of believing that at the end Jesus will come in such a way as to extort faith or stampede men into belief…but can it be that anyone will reject him even at the last? That is a speculation to which the New Testament does not lend itself."

Universalism is appealing to some. There is no doubt of that. After the 1967 InterVarsity Christian Fellowship Missionary Convention at Urbana, Illinois, a questionnaire was sent to more than eight thousand delegates. Sixty-seven percent of the delegates responded! According to the survey only thirty-five percent of the delegates felt that people were lost apart from receiving the gospel. Most of these would consider themselves evangelical Christians. Of people who had been accepted by mission boards to go out as missionaries, only forty-five percent felt that persons were lost apart from the gospel. Of those delegates responding who were actually missionaries, only sixty-two percent believed that persons were lost apart from the Gospel (Price 1976, 27-28). This is frightening to Bible-believing Christians.

Bernard Ramm, once a leading American theologian, gave a significant statement concerning the growth of universalism:

The first cause for Universalism gaining a new foothold in contemporary Christianity is that the task of world evangelism seems so hopeless. It was the burning hope of the great missionary statesmen of the nineteenth century that the world could be evangelized in one generation if each convert would win but one more convert; in the space of one generation the entire world would hear of the Gospel of Christ [quoted by Price 1976, 27].

The situation appears far differently to the missionary statesmen of the twentieth century. Missionary evangelism proceeds at a slow rate. Only one-half percent of Japan's millions are Christian. The figures are equally discouraging for India, China, and Indonesia.

But there is a factor more discouraging than the slow process of missionary evangelism. That factor is the world population explosion. Modern medicine and sanitation introduced to Africa and Asia are having a boomerang effect. These pagan populations are literally booming and that at a geometric ratio. India alone increases from twelve to fourteen million a year! The population of the earth at the year 2000 will be fantastically large. The problem of Christianity is no longer whether it shall reach these people. Rather it is in danger being engulfed by them.

Evangelists and missionary statesmen are faced with a decision: Do we write these countless people out of the kingdom and proclaim them lost? Or in an act of Christian generosity, do we write them all in with a doctrine of universalism? If we write them out, then this reduces Christianity to a small band among the earth's billions. It also means that the lives of the vast throngs of heathen are meaningless, for meaning is found only in Christ. To write them all in means that every life is meaningful even though lived without a consciousness of the saving work of Christ. Thus, universalism saves significance for the Christian churches and the millions of lives upon the face of the globe.

If all are in fact redeemed by Christ, then evangelism is not winning people to Christ. It is the process of *informing* them that they are in fact redeemed and ought to start living accordingly. "The missionary does not bring Christ to India or Africa for Christ is already there being the universal Savior of all men. The missionary comes to announce the universal lordship of Christ and summons men to acknowledge it in their lives" (Ramm 1964, quoted by Price 1976, 23-24).

The theological arguments put forth in favor of universalism all deal with the nature of God—God's love, God's omnipotence, God's eternality, and God's justice. Let us look at omnipotence and love together, because they are usually considered together. William Dalton said, "The God of the New Testament is not half-saving, half-punishing: he is the God of salvation . . . if he can save all men then he will save all men" (1977,81). Nels Ferre, a well-known American theologian, said: "The logic of the situation is simple, either God could not or would not save all. If he could not he is not sovereign: then not all things are possible with God (Matthew 19:26 KJV). If he would not, again the New Testament is wrong, for it openly claims that he would have all to be saved (I Timothy 2:4 KJV). Nor would he be totally good" [1971, 118].

The third attribute of God which universalists consider is God's eternality. Universalists argue that God is not limited by time and this means that his love is not limited by time. They therefore believe that because God's love is eternal and God is eternal, ultimately all will be saved.

The fourth attribute of God which universalists call upon is God's justice. They contend that because God is just he cannot allow any of his creatures to be eternally lost. Though many universalists believe in Hell, they do not believe in an eternal Hell. Ferre said, "Heaven can be heaven only when it has emptied hell" (1971, 119).

A number of Scripture passages are used by universalists. John Sanders noted that the passages used to support universalism fall into five categories: (1) those that affirm God's desire to save all people (1 Timothy 2:4; 4:10; 2 Peter 3:9); (2) those that proclaim the unlimited atonement of Christ (1 John 2:2; Hebrews 2:9; Titus 2:11; 2 Corinthians 5:19); (3) those that articulate the implications of the universal atoning work of Jesus (John 12:32; Colossians 1 20; Romans 5:12-19; 9:23; 11:32).

The fourth set of biblical texts refers to the "consummation" of God's plan of salvation in which all people are finally redeemed. This is called restorationism (Acts 3:19-21; Philippians 2:9-11; 1 Corinthians15:22-28). The last group of texts refers to damnation and separation. These passages speak of two classes of people, the saved and the lost, the sheep and the goats. Universalists understand them according to the interpretation of the Scriptures listed above. Universalists do not believe in eternal damnation. They believe that the New Testament affirms the reconciliation of God's creatures.

I do not believe universalism is biblical and I am sure that acceptance of this view will destroy evangelism. If everyone will eventually be saved, why bother to witness? Also, how can one possibly ignore the clear teachings by Jesus on the fate of the lost? Universalism should be refuted at every opportunity!

11.B. PLURALISM

Pluralism is the idea that all religions provide a way to God. An interesting question was raised in a conference held in 1994:

Could the world religions confer full legitimacy on such an organization in concert with all the other religions and with the various forms of secularism? That would mean, of course, each religion's de facto acceptance of the coequal status of other religions and even secular humanism itself approached as a major world religion [Boston Research Center 1994].

John Hick, fellow at the Institute for Advanced Research in the Humanities, Birmingham University (UK), and Professor Emeritus at Claremont Graduate School, was a widely known and influential pluralist. I shall use him as an example of pluralism. In Birmingham there was a sizeable group of people representing non-Christian traditions—Muslims, Sikhs, and Hindu communities as well as some Buddhist groups. Hick became much involved in many community organizations that put him into contact with these religious groups. Hick wrote:

In these places of worship I soon realized what is obvious enough once noticed, yet momentous in its implications. . . . God is known in the synagogues as Adonai, the Lord God of Abraham, Isaac, and Jacob; in the mosques as Allah Rahman Rahim, God beneficent and merciful; in the Sikh gurud waras as god, who is Father, Lover, Master, and the Great Giver, referred to as war guru; and in the Hindu temples as Vishnu, Krishnam (an incarnation of Vishnu, Rama, Shiva, and many other gods and goddesses, all of whom are seen as manifestations of the ultimate reality of Brahman); and in the Christian churches as the triune God, Father, Son, and Holy Spirit, and yet all these communities agree that there can ultimately only be one God! [1995, 38].

Hick believed "that the God-figures of the great theistic religions are different human awarenesses of the Ultimate, rather than the traditional Christian view that we alone have a true knowledge of God" (1995, 38). Hick argued that all religions have a mixture of good and evil. When he speaks of evil in the Christian religion he talks of the European class system over several centuries and the greedy use of the earth's non-renewable resources. He uses several other arguments, but his point is that it cannot be claimed properly that the fruits of the Christian faith in human life are superior to those of the other world religions.

What about salvation? Hick argued:

If we define salvation as being forgiven and accepted by God because of Jesus' death on the cross, then it becomes a tautology that Christianity alone knows and is able to preach the source of salvation. [1995, 43].

Hicks believed that salvation was a term most often found in Christianity. The term *redemption* would be familiar to many Christians and Jews but Muslims are more familiar with the idea of submitting oneself to God. Eastern religions focus on the concept of liberation or even enlightenment. Hicks therefore preferred the compound term *salvation/liberation* in his writings. [1995, 43-44].

For Hick to come to this place he has had to revise his thinking on the incarnation and also on the Trinity and atonement. He does not believe that Jesus is God incarnate nor that Jesus had two complete natures, one human and the other divine. Those who accept pluralism, I believe, must of necessity deny the incarnation, the doctrine of the Triune God, and the necessity of the atoning death of Jesus. There is then no need for evangelism! To accept Hicks' view, one would have to make a scrapbook of the New Testament! I believe that pluralism is as dangerous as the teaching of universalism.

11.C. INCLUSIVISM

Inclusivists believe that salvation is universally accessible apart from evangelization. Hick wrote, "[Inclusivism] probably represents the nearest approach to consensus among Christian thinkers today" (1993, 88).

A leading proponent of inclusivism was Clark Pinnock, who taught at McMaster Divinity College in Hamilton, Ontario. He had also taught at a number of leading evangelical institutions over the years.

Pinnock noted:

Inclusivism celebrates two central theological truths. The first is a particularity axiom that says God has revealed himself definitively and has acted redemptively on behalf of the whole human race through the Incarnation. The second is a universality axiom that says God loves sinners and wants to save them all. The challenge to theology is to do justice to both these truths and not allow one to cancel out the other. Conservative theology tends to deny universality and liberalism rejects particularity [1995, 141].

Inclusivism is rapidly gaining popularity. Pinnock noted several reasons for this: (1) "Hope attracts and Inclusivism genders hope. Christians want to believe that grace will prove stronger than sin in the flow of history." (2) "Inclusivism relieves us of those dark features of the tradition that suggest that (at worst) God plays favorites or (at best) inexplicably restricts his grace so that whole groups are excluded from any possibility of salvation. More and more Christians are refusing to believe these notions." (3) "Inclusivism appeals because of its honest willingness to acknowledge sanctity in persons and religions other than Christian. Too many of us have encountered saintly persons of other faiths to deny that the religious communities behind them are in a state of some openness to God." (4) "A fourth source of attraction lies in the way inclusivism offers a more coherent version of orthodoxy" (1995, 101-2). Inclusivism affirms the universality of God's will to save and does this "without reducing 'God' to a vague Kantian in certain forms of pluralism, a Reality that none can define and that replaces the historic confession of the triune God" (1995, 102). It is the sort of middle road between exclusivism and pluralism.

Pinnock does believe that Christ is the Savior of all people, but they do not all come to him in the same way. He believes that the Holy Spirit is at work on the inside and the outside of the churches (1995, 105). I do not want to misinterpret Pinnock. Let me quote again: "Not a scholar of comparative religions, I welcome the *Saiva*

Siddhanta literature of Hinduism, which celebrates a personal God of love, and the emphasis on grace seen in the Japanese Shin-Shu Amid a sect. I also respect the Buddha as a righteous man (Matthew 10:41) and Mohammed as a prophet figure in the style of the Old Testament" (1995, 110).

Pinnock believes that people are saved through faith, though I am not sure exactly faith in what or whom. He contends that it is in faith in the creator God. He speaks of believers who are not Christians or believers who have not had "messianic salvation."

The idea of the cosmic Christ is not new. Interestingly enough, Bishop K. H. Ting of China has embraced the idea of the cosmic Christ. In an article in the China Theological Review, Bishop Ting said:

Increasingly, we cast off the pedantry over the human and divine natures of Christ. Beyond the human/ divine issue, our theological thinking is liberated and deepened and finds greater cohesion in terms of Christ's cosmic nature. The cosmic nature of Christ is the Christology to be found in the New Testament books of Colossians, Ephesians, and the Gospel of John. . . . I am not trying to suggest that the phrase "cosmic Christ" has entered into the common vocabulary of the mass of theological workers, but it can be said that increasing numbers of Christians are encountering this Christ by various paths and, in their own ways, are bringing people to know and adore this Christ [1993].

In an article titled "The Cosmic Christ and Theological Thinking," published in the *China Theological Review* in 1996, a third year student at Nanjing Union Theological Seminary, Qiu Wet, said:

Bishop K. H. Ting's thinking on the Cosmic Christ represents the highest achievement of Chinese Christian theological reflection at present. As Bishop Ting has himself said, this reflection "has resulted from the dash of historical transformation with traditional beliefs."

The comparatively long historical encounter between the Chinese people and Christian thought began with Nestorianism in the Tang Dynasty and extends over a thousand years. Signs of God's salvific activity and traces of Christ's presence can be felt in all cultures [1996, 11].

These teachings are extremely detrimental to evangelism. Key biblical texts used by the inclusivists are Luke 15; 23:34; John 1:9; 12:32; 1 Timothy 1:15; 4:10; 2 Peter 3:9. A second group of texts deals with God's dealing with Gentiles outside the covenant with

Israel. These include Genesis 1:26-28, a covenant made between God and the human race, not between God and Israel. Another such passage is Genesis 9:8-19; also Genesis 12:3. The case of the Syrian military man Naaman is considered an inclusivist passage. Isaiah 45:1-7 telling of God working through Cyrus King of Persia is noted. Others have cited Jonah 1:16; Amos 1:1-2, 8; Obadiah 15; Nahum 1:2; Zechariah 9:1. Pinnock noted that Jesus found "great faith" in the Canaanite woman, Matthew 15:21-28, and in the Roman centurion, Matthew 8:10.

Probably the most noted Scripture passage used by inclusivists is the account in Acts 10 of Cornelius and Peter. But if one reads carefully this passage, it seems obvious that this "devout man, one that feared God with all his house, which gave much alms to the people, and prayed to God always" (Acts 10:2) needed to *hear the gospel!*

I am reminded again of Paul's word to the Romans in chapter 10:8-17 (KJV).

But what saith it? The word is nigh thee, even in thy mouth, and in thy heart: that is, the word of faith, which we preach; That if thou shalt confess with the mouth the Lord Jesus, and shalt believe in thine heart that God hath raised him from the dead, thou shalt be saved. For with the heart man believeth unto righteousness; and with the mouth confession is made unto salvation. For the scripture saith, 'Whosoever believeth on him shall not be ashamed.' For there is no difference between the Jew and the Greek; for the same Lord over all is rich unto all that call upon him. For whosoever shall call upon the name of the Lord shall be saved. How then shall they call on him in whom they have not believed? And how shall they believe in him of whom they have not heard? And how shall they hear without a preacher? And how shall they preach, except they be sent? As it is written, 'How beautiful are the feet of them that preach the gospel of peace, and bring glad tidings of good things!' But they have not all obeyed the gospel. For Esaias saith, 'Lord, who hath believed our report?' So then faith cometh by hearing, and hearing by the word of God.

Inclusivism sounds good but will destroy evangelism.

11.D. UNIVERSAL OPPORTUNITY BEFORE DEATH

A number of people in our day believe that God will see to it that all unevangelized persons who seek him will be able to hear the gospel so they may be able to decide for or against Christ. Some believe God will send the message only through human agents. Others believe that he may send it through dreams or angels. Some believe that God will send the gospel message to every unevangelized person, but others do not. Some biblical texts to which these appeal are Hebrews 11:6, John 4:23, Acts 8 (the story of the Ethiopian eunuch), Acts 10 (Cornelius), Genesis 20 (the story of Abimelech), Daniel 2 (Nebuchadnezzar), and Ananias in Acts 9:10.

Those who hold this view believe that general revelation is not sufficient for salvation but simply to help people to see that there is a God. Those who maintain this position believe that one must have specific knowledge of Christ in order to be saved. They believe that no person will seek God unless God has extended grace to that one. Some, such as Robertson McQuilkin (President of Columbia International University) believe that those who respond to the light that they have will receive the light that they need. Those who hold this view believe that no one has an opportunity to be evangelized after death.

There are some, notably Roman Catholics, who believe that the unevangelized will be given an opportunity to be saved at the moment of death. This has been called the "final option" theory.

Others hold a "middle knowledge" theory. "Proponents of this view hold that God has three types of knowledge: (1) He knows all the possibilities that could happen in any state of affairs, (2) He knows all that would happen in any state of affairs, if one of the conditions were different in any way, and (3) He knows all that will actually happen" (Sanders 1992, 168). There are two groups who advocate "middle knowledge" in regard to unevangelized people. One group believes that God will save unevangelized people who would have accepted Christ had they had the opportunity of hearing the gospel. The second group believes that God possesses "middle knowledge" but they do not believe He has to use it to save the unevangelized. They believe that God supplies enough grace for every individual to be saved but that no person can be saved apart from hearing about Jesus Christ from a human agent. (Much of the information on universal evangelization before death was obtained from Sanders 1992, 151-175.)

11.E. ESCHATOLOGICAL OR POSTMORTEM EVANGELISM

Some people believe the idea that individuals may receive, after death, an opportunity to hear about Christ and to accept or reject him. Major biblical texts for this group are Mark 16:15-16; Matthew 10:32-33, 12:40; John 5:25-29; 15:22; Hosea 13:14; Ephesians 4:8-10; Philippians 2:10; Revelation 1:18; 5:13. Perhaps the most notable text is 1 Peter 3:18-4:6.

A basic rule of Scripture interpretation comes into play. Let Scripture interpret Scripture. If a text seems to teach something in contradiction to a preponderance of Scripture, go with the teaching of the majority. The preponderance of Scripture teaches no opportunity for salvation after physical death. Eschatological, or postmortem evangelism, cuts the nerve and kills the motivation of evangelism.

11.F. THE MODERN FAITH MOVEMENT

There is abroad in our world a different gospel. Some who claim to follow Christ attempt to manipulate God. They tell God what to do. They give him instructions as to what they desire and claim these things as their rights. They also claim that physical healing is in the atonement of Jesus Christ and that God does not want any of his children to be sick. Both of these teachings are in error. God is God and cannot be manipulated nor instructed. As Paul wrote in 1 Corinthians 2:16 (KJV), "For who hath known the mind of the Lord, that he may instruct him?" One should ponder the words of God to Job in Job 38-40.

This modern faith movement, sometimes called "health and wealth" thinking, also cuts the nerve of evangelism. Our task is not to tell people they may be healthy and wealthy but to tell them they may be forgiven of their sins and brought into fellowship with a holy God through the sacrifice of Jesus Christ the Son of God.

I believe that all these views pose a real danger to evangelism. If one adopts any one of these views, it seems to me that evangelism will cease to be a priority, because each of them cuts the cord of missions and evangelism. There is a theological position which I hold to be the biblical view. It deserves more attention than I will be able to give in this article.

11.G. RESTRICTIVISM (EXCLUSIVISM)

The view held by most evangelical Christians for centuries and still held by many today is that of restrictivism or exclusivism. Those who hold this view believe that God does not provide salvation to those who fail to hear of Jesus and who fail to come to faith in him before they die. I am using an outline from John Sanders in his book, *No Other Name*, pages 42-48.

First, some biblical texts affirm the particularity and exclusiveness of salvation in Jesus Christ: Acts 4:12; 1 Corinthians 3:11 ("For other foundation can no man lay than that is laid, which is Jesus Christ"); John 14:6; John 17:3 ("And this is life eternal, that they might know thee the only true God, and Jesus Christ, whom thou hast sent"); 1 John 5:11-12 ("And this is the record, that God hath given to us eternal life, and this life is in his Son. He that hath the Son hath life; and he that hath not the Son of God hath not life").

Second, general revelation does not provide a means of salvation. There are Scriptures which show the sinfulness of all persons and the hopelessness of life without Jesus Christ. Romans 1-3 very clearly states this. Paul argued that Gentiles have turned away from the light of general revelation (1:20) and conscience (2:15) and that Jews have refused to follow the light of special revelation (2:23). This places all under sin and guilty before God (3:9). In Romans 1, Paul said that people without Christ are darkened in their understanding, excluded from the life of God, because of the ignorance that is in them, because of the hardness of their heart.

Third, commitment to Christ must occur during one's lifetime. Mark 1:14-15 (KJV) says, "Now after that John was put in prison, Jesus came into Galilee, preaching the gospel of the kingdom of God, and saying, The time is fulfilled and the kingdom of God is at hand. Repent and believe the gospel." John 3:36 (KJV) says, "He that believeth on the Son hath everlasting life: and he that believeth not the Son shall not see life; but the wrath of God abideth on him." 1 John 2:23 (KJV) says, "Whosoever denieth the Son, the same hath not the Father: he that acknowledgeth the Son hath the Father also." In Romans 10:9-10 (KJV) Paul stated, "That if thou shalt confess with thy mouth the Lord Jesus, and shalt believe in thine heart that God hath raised him from the dead, thou shalt be saved. For with the heart man believeth unto righteousness; and with the mouth confession is made unto salvation." In Romans 10:14 (KJV) Paul said, "How then shall they call on him in whom they have not believed? and how shall they believe in him of whom they have not heard? and how shall they hear without a preacher?" In Romans 10:17 (KJV) he wrote, "So then faith cometh by hearing, and hearing by the word of God."

The example of Cornelius is given by several groups, but I believe the correct interpretation is this: Cornelius was a "God fearer," that is, he stood in awe of the God of Israel. An angel had told Cornelius that he should send for Simon Peter, "who shall tell thee words, whereby thou and all thy house shall be saved" (Acts 11:14 KJV). That is, though Cornelius feared God, he was not saved until he heard the gospel message and trusted in Jesus Christ.

Fourth, the unevangelized deserve condemnation. Paul makes this clear in Romans 1-3. The position of restrictivism provides a great incentive for missions. If people who have never heard of Jesus and therefore do not trust in him are lost forever, it is essential that those of us who know and love Jesus Christ get the message to them. Someone once said to Charles Haddon Spurgeon, the great English preacher, "Mr. Spurgeon, I cannot believe that people who have never heard of Jesus cannot be saved." Spurgeon answered, "I cannot believe that those of us who know and love him will not go and tell them." This constitutes the great heartthrob of missions. We must get the message to sinful people that God loves them, that he has sent his Son to die for them, that he will save them from their sins and bring them into the family of God if they repent and commit their lives to Jesus Christ the Lord.

In this day of "easy-believism," of universalism, of pluralism, of inclusivism, of "health and wealth" preaching, it is essential that we who have been redeemed by the Lord Jesus be faithful to the Word of God. I believe that Paul's word to Timothy is God's word to us: "Be instant in season, out of season . . . do the work of an evangelist" (2 Timothy 4:2, 5 KJV).

People are lost without Jesus Christ. They are condemned. Paul wrote: "But if our gospel be hid, it is hid to them that are lost: In whom the god of this world hath blinded the minds of them which believe not, lest the light of the glorious gospel of Christ, who is the image of God, should shine unto them" (2 Corinthians 4:3-4 KJV).

Let us care, let us dare, let us share. Good news cannot be lived and cannot be received by osmosis. It must be declared!

I am reminded of the ones of whom John wrote: "And they overcame him by the blood of the Lamb, and by the word of their testimony; and they loved not their lives unto the death" (Revelation 12:11 KJV). They were saved by the blood of the Lamb, they were witnesses by the word of their testimony, and they witnessed even if it brought death. May this be true of us!

WORKS CITED IN THIS CHAPTER

Boston Research Center for the 21st Century: Cambridge, MA, 1994. The United Nations and the World's Religions.

Dalton, William. *Salvation and Damnation*. Butler, WI: Clergy Book Service, 1977.

Ferre, Nels. *Evil and the Christian Faith*. Freeport, New York: Books for Libraries Press, 1971.

Hick, John. "A Pluralist View." In *More Than One Way?* Ed. D. L. Okholm and T. R. Phillips. Grand Rapids: Zondervan, 1995.

_____. *The Metaphor of God Incarnate*. Louisville: Westminster/John Knox, 1993.

Newman, Albert Henry. In *A Manual of Church History*, vol. 1. Philadelphia: American Baptist Publication Society, 1904.

Niles, D. T. *Upon the Earth*. New York: McGraw-Hill, 1962.

Pinnock, Clark H., "An Inclusivist View." In *More Than One Way?* Ed. D. L. Okholm and T. R. Phillips. Grand Rapids: Zondervan, 1995.

Price, Wendell W. *Contemporary Problems of Evangelism*. Harrisburg, PA: Christian Publications, 1976.

Ramm, Bernard. "Will All Men Finally Be Saved?" Eternity (August 1964) quoted by Wendell W. Price, *Contemporary Problems of Evangelism.*

Sanders, John. *No Other Name*, Grand Rapids: Eerdmans, 1992.

Ting, K. H. "Foundation for Theological Education in Southeast."

"Asia." *China Theological Review* 8, 1993.

Wei, Qiu. "The Cosmic Christ and Theological Thinking." *China Theological Review* 11, 1996.

CHAPTER 12

MUSLIM EVANGELISM

With the increasing contact between the Christian West and the Muslim East and Pacific Rim, more emphasis needs to be given to sharing the gospel with Muslims. Some Muslim evangelism approaches require a thorough understanding of the Quran (the Holy Book of the Muslim religion). Since this would be considered impractical for many Christians, simple Muslim evangelistic methods are to be preferred.

Using the testimony of Adam and the book of Genesis, you can begin a witnessing conversation with a Muslim. Some Muslims are very superficial in their knowledge of their own faith, so a detailed argument may not be productive. However, a casual conversation about a topic in both the Bible and the Quran can be a bridge for the gospel. You should be aware that because of cultural differences, it is often best for men to share the gospel with men and for women to share the gospel with women. We can use the Adam Method and incorporate it into the outline that we have already learned.

The Adam Method uses Genesis 3 and Adam and should be done in a conversation format. The person witnessing could begin with, "Do you know in the Quran about the prophet Adam?" (Adam is called a prophet in the Quran.) They will usually answer that they do know about him. Continue, "The Holy Book says that Adam sinned against God. It took one sin to separate the holy prophet from God. We have sinned more than one time, and we are not a prophet. Adam hid himself and tried, through his own works, to make himself right with God, but God rejected his efforts. Only the work of God in covering Adam's sin could make him right with God. If the works of a prophet could not make him righteous before God, how will our works make us righteous before God? Adam needed a 'covering' for his sin. The Bible says that God has provided a covering for sin and that covering is the gift of God through Jesus Christ."[41]

1. The Introduction. Begin a gospel conversation with a Muslim. If you know an Arabic greeting, you might use it to start the conversation.

Example: Arabic greeting. You can say, *"as-salaam 'alaykum,"* which means, "peace be upon you." The response to this greeting is, *"wa 'alaykum as-salaam,"* which means, "and also with you."

Assess the person: Are they well-informed of their faith? Are they a cultural Muslim? Are they Folk-Islam (a mixture of animism and Islam)?

2. A Diagnostic Question. "Do you know in the Quran about the prophet Adam?" Continue with the Adam Method conversation.

3. The Gospel Presentation.
    (1) Salvation Needed (Scripture)
    (2) Salvation Provided (Scripture)
    (3) Salvation Accepted (Scripture)

4. The Invitation. Ask the person to receive Christ as Lord and Savior.

5. Follow Up.
    If they say NO . . . .
    If they say YES . . . .

NOTE: Since you may meet resistance on the first encounter in sharing the gospel, keep the door open for future conversations. Remember that Jesus loves them and wants them to know Him. Also, be careful about delaying too long in building a relationship. After a relationship has developed, it may be difficult to bring up the gospel, and you can risk them thinking that you didn't really care about them—you befriended them under false pretenses because you wanted to share your religion with them. Honesty and transparency make for better friendships.

A good resource for Muslim evangelism is the book *Any-3: Anyone, Anywhere, Any Time.* The book is written by Mike Shipman who served with the International Mission Board among Muslims in Asia for many years. The methods are field tested, and the book is recommended by a number of workers who serve in similar areas.[42]

CHAPTER 13

THE GOSPEL INVITATION

13.A. BIBLICAL EXAMPLES OF A CALL FOR A DECISION

Extending a call for a decision after the presentation of the gospel is thoroughly biblical. A call for a decision must include the call to repent of sin and the call to turn to Jesus as Lord and Savior. A quick survey of the Bible can easily prove the overwhelming evidence that calling for a decision is proper and necessary.

1. Moses called for a decision. In Exodus 32:26 it says, "Then Moses stood in the gate of the camp, and said, 'Whoever is for the Lord, come to me!' And all the sons of Levi gathered together to him." (Exodus 32:26 NASB)

2. Joshua called for a decision. He said, "If it is disagreeable in your sight to serve the Lord, choose for yourselves today whom you will serve: whether the gods which your fathers served which were beyond the River, or the gods of the Amorites in whose land you are now living; but as for me and my house, we will serve the Lord." (Joshua 24:15 NASB)

3. The prophet Elijah called for an immediate decision. The Scripture says, "Elijah came near to all the people and said, 'How long will you hesitate between two opinions? If the Lord is God, follow Him; but if Baal, follow him.' But the people did not answer him a word." (1 Kings 18:21 NASB)

4. The Lord Jesus called for a decision. Jesus said, "Come to Me, all who are weary and heavy-laden, and I will give you rest. Take my yoke upon you and learn from Me, for I am gentle and humble in heart, and you will find rest for your souls. For My yoke is easy and My burden is light." (Matthew 11:28-30 NASB)

5. The Apostle Peter spoke of a decision. "And with many other words he solemnly testified and kept on exhorting them, saying, 'Be saved from this perverse generation.'" (Acts 2:40 NASB)

6. The Apostle Paul asked for a response from the lost. "That if you confess with your mouth Jesus as Lord, and believe in your heart that God raised Him from the dead, you will be saved; for with the heart a person believes, resulting in righteousness, and with the mouth he confesses, resulting in salvation." (Romans 10:9-10 NASB)

7. The Apostle John in the book of Revelation calls for a decision for Christ. "The Spirit and the Bride say, 'Come.' And let the one who hears say, 'Come.' And let the one who wishes to take the water of life without cost." (Revelation 22:17 NASB)

13.B. THE PROPER METHODS FOR EXTENDING AN INVITATION

An invitation is the biblical conclusion to any presentation of God's truth. It is the logical end to a gospel witness, and it is the normal conclusion of an evangelistic sermon. In reality, every time the Word of God is preached, an invitation to respond must be given. The sermon is not a story but a message from God that demands a response from sinners.

The moments given for people to ponder their response to the message from God's Word can often lead to numerous benefits. This time allows God the Holy Spirit to do a deep work in the hearts of those listening. Conviction of sin is deepened among the unsaved and a call to righteous living is at work among the saved.

The call for a decision must be direct and clear. "Would you like to accept Jesus Christ as your personal Lord and Savior right now?" It is as important to be specific on time as it is to be specific as to the decision. It is not manipulation to ask someone to make an immediate decision; it is biblical. In fact, the last chapter of the last book of the Bible, the book of Revelation, extends an invitation. John said, "The Spirit and the Bride say, 'Come.' And let the one who hears say, 'Come.' And let the one who is thirsty come; let the one who wishes take the water of life without cost" (Revelation 22:17 NASB).

The following steps will help to guide in making your invitations biblical and effective:

1. The invitation must be the logical extension of the message. It should not be an abrupt departure from what has previously been said. If you keep each message tied to Jesus and the cross, you will not have to leap to the gospel in order to make an effective invitation.

2. Be clear, concise, and biblical. Exactly what are you asking people to do? Avoid terms and phrases that only an active church member would understand. Saying phrases like, "move your letter," will be difficult for a new church attender to comprehend. Is the decision biblical? Are the commitments you are asking the audience to make clearly from the Bible?

3. Never manipulate people. God the Holy Spirit is fully capable of controlling the invitation by convicting people of their sin and the need of repentance. If the Word has been taught and preached accurately and with power, the invitation will have power. Although you do not have to avoid all emotion, be sensitive to using emotional stories at the time of the invitation. Let the Spirit do the moving.

4. Give a sinner's prayer as a part of the invitation. Modeling a prayer of repentance ensures that a lost person knows precisely what to do to repent and turn to the Lord. Another benefit is that the repetition of the prayer will train regular church members in evangelism. When an attender has heard a prayer to repent and believe on numerous occasions, when they have an opportunity to share their faith, they can remember the prayer as a part of the conclusion of their witness for Christ.

5. Have trained counselors available at all times. Even if the pastor is extending an invitation, he should have people available to take the ones who respond during the invitation to a place for detailed counseling. Avoid presenting people immediately in a public service because this can place pressure on the counselors to assess quickly someone's spiritual condition. When someone presents themselves for counseling, a good question to ask is, "Why have you come today?" It allows for them to speak of what the Holy Spirit is doing in their life.

6. Do you have to walk down an aisle to make a decision? Not necessarily, but it is a good plan. Public confessions of faith are important even though for some people it may be a difficult step. Some churches will allow people interested in making decisions to approach church staff or other designated leaders after a service. However a church does their decision time, it should be well-organized, and the steps to contacting someone should be clear. If you say, "Find a staff person," and the

staff have to leave soon for other responsibilities, then you will make it difficult for people who want to make a decision. I preached in one church and was asked not to give an invitation; the staff would do any counseling after the service. After the service, a person came up to me and wanted to join the church. The two of us went looking for staff, but the only people we could find were the sound technicians. I took her information and told her I would get it to the right people. Much later, a staff member told me that I should have just told her to go to the church website and go to the prospective member page.

We need a "no prospect left behind" mentality and should rehearse as church staff and the counseling team how people make decisions, how they will be counseled, and how they will begin immediate discipleship. Have a plan, explain the plan each and every service to the congregation, and execute that plan!

7. A pastor should regularly have special services where the main focus is on evangelism. This type of service can easily be incorporated into an exegetical sermon series or used on a special occasion. These types of services are excellent occasions to explain in detail about the biblical necessity of believer's baptism and church membership. "Therefore everyone who confesses Me before men, I will also confess him before the Father who is in heaven" (Matthew 10:32 NASB).

8. Sample sinner's prayer. While some may criticize using a sinner's prayer, it is an effective evangelistic tool. The Lord Jesus gave us a model prayer even though we are not expected to pray that way in every situation. In a culture with little or no Christian influence, you cannot assume that someone knows how to pray, especially if they have never truly prayed before. Parts of this prayer are modeled from what Dr. Adrian Rogers, longtime pastor of Bellevue Baptist Church in Memphis, Tennessee, used in his invitations.

Dear Lord, I know that I am a sinner, I know that I have done wrong. I believe in You, Jesus; I believe You died on the cross and rose from the dead for me. Forgive me of my sins and save me right now, Lord Jesus. Become the Lord of my life, I give my all to You.

If you lead in a sinner's prayer, you must make sure to emphasize that this is for people who are old enough to understand their sin and need of Christ. It is for those who have never before trusted in Christ as Savior. After praying the sinner's prayer, you should ask people to declare publicly that they are following Christ as Lord and Savior.

Hear the words of Dr. Adrian Rogers, longtime pastor of Bellevue Baptist Church in Memphis, Tennessee:

> Be courageous when you give an invitation. You know why some men will not give an invitation? Because they are afraid that there will be no response. And because they're afraid there will be no response, they won't give an invitation. They're so anxious to keep people from saying no, they won't give them a chance to say yes. You have to be courageous to give an invitation because it costs, it hurts.[43]

CHAPTER 14

EVANGELISM STRATEGY FOR CHURCHES

14.A. DEFINITION OF EVANGELISM STRATEGY FOR CHURCHES

The Greek word *ekklesia* often translated "church" in English Bibles denotes a community, not a building. Further, the word *ekklesia* is overwhelmingly used to denote a church in a geographic location such as the church at Philippi or the church at Thessalonika. The few times that *ekklesia* is not used geographically it is used in a generic sense, such as discussing church discipline (Matthew 18). The New Testament church is a local, called by God, assembly of believers. The New Testament uses the illustration of a body to describe the relation and function of a church. Jesus is aptly described as the head of the church (Colossians 1:18). The members of the church are the body, gifted by the Holy Spirit to work together to honor Christ (1 Corinthians 12; Romans 12:6-8).

In his pivotal book of a previous generation, Donald McGavran claimed that churches grow in three ways. The first way a church grows is through *biological growth* which describes the children of church members growing up, accepting Christ, and joining a local church. The second type of church growth is *transfer growth*. Transfer growth occurs when members of one congregation join another congregation. While this can benefit the recipient congregation by multiplying its leadership base, it is not Great Commission growth. The third type of growth is *conversion growth*. People with no church connections who come to Christ are an essential growth if the Great Commission is to be accomplished.[44]

Evangelism results in discipled believers who congregate together to honor Jesus and take the gospel to the nations. Believers reproduce to birth new believers and churches reproduce to birth new churches.

14.B. THE REPRODUCING STRATEGY: EVANGELISM AND ENLISTMENT

According to Dr. Brad Roderick, longtime mission strategist, people can be seen as prospects for evangelism or as prospects to do evangelism. This approach incorporates the true biblical view of discipleship. Evangelism results in disciples which results in churches. Churches then produce evangelists who make disciples who plant churches. A church evangelism strategy is really a Great Commission strategy. Revelation 7:9 (NASB) states, "After these things I looked, and behold, a great multitude which no one could count, from every nation and all tribes and peoples and tongues, standing before the throne and before the Lamb, clothed in white robes, and palm branches were in their hands."[45]

When you encounter a person, you should see them as a prospect for evangelism. This begins a process whereby they move from seeking entry into the kingdom of God through salvation. Once they enter, they begin a journey of discipleship and, hopefully, leadership training (this is for all believers, not necessarily church officers). From leadership training, believers should move to equipping and expansion. These believers reproduce themselves through evangelism and they reproduce their church through church planting. This process is enhanced by the calling of special servants of local churches by God the Holy Spirit.

> *And He gave some as apostles, and some as prophets, and some as evangelists, and some as pastors and teachers, for the equipping of the saints for the work of service, to the building up of the body of Christ; until we all attain   to the unity of the faith, and of the knowledge of the Son of God, to a mature man, to the measure of the stature which belongs to the fullness of Christ. (Ephesians 4:11-13 NASB)*

So an evangelism strategy for churches incorporates the process of reproduction. This reproduction is not local or regional, it is global. A church maintains its scriptural fidelity by its Great Commission activity.[46]

14.C. DIFFERENT TYPES OF EVANGELISM

Three words can be used to describe various aspects of personal and church evangelism: *presence*, *proclamation*, and *persuasion*. While a danger exists in simplifying evangelism into one-word concepts, some benefit may be derived in looking on these ideas for illustrative purposes.

The first type of evangelism is presence evangelism. Simply put, evangelism occurs by a Christian being in a certain place. Since no verbal witness is usually ascribed to presence evangelism, it can be asserted that this is really not New Testament evangelism at all. The Lord Jesus went about teaching and preaching, not just existing. While a godly lifestyle is important in maintaining the credibility to witness, this is not enough to bring people to saving faith in Christ. How can a lost person learn that the Son of God came and died for sin on the cross and rose again on the third day just by observing someone else? Also, since Christians usually are grouped into certain parts of the world, vast areas would never know the gospel because no Christians are in those places.

The second phrase, proclamation evangelism, is best described as declaring the facts of the gospel. Media ministries often serve as examples of proclamation evangelism. The truths of the gospel are broadcast, but no interpersonal interaction takes place. This view of evangelism represents something that is good, but this is not the best form of evangelism for Great Commission fulfillment.

The third type of evangelism is persuasion evangelism. In this view, human interaction is combined with the gospel message. Or, in other words, the gospel is presented one person at a time. Acts 28:23 (NASB) says, "When they had set a day for Paul, they came to him at his lodging in large numbers; and he was explaining to them by solemnly testifying about the kingdom of God and trying to persuade them concerning Jesus, from both the Law of Moses and from the prophets, from morning until evening." Persuasion evangelism is also emphasized in 2 Corinthians 5:20 (NASB): "Therefore, we are ambassadors for Christ, as though God were making an appeal through us; we beg you on behalf of Christ, be reconciled to God."

14.D. THE CULTURE OF CHURCH EVANGELISM

The importance of vision and pastoral leadership in evangelism cannot be overstated. A church's best evangelism program is usually what the pastor uses for his own personal evangelism. In his book *Total Church Life*, Darrell Robinson gives an excellent example of biblical and pastoral evangelistic vision. Robinson's approach is that everything in the life of a local, New Testament church is related to evangelism. Anything in church not aiding the evangelistic efforts of the congregation should be discarded. The threefold outline of *Total Church Life* is, Exalt the Savior, Equip the Saints, and Evangelize the Sinners. Robinson stated, "The greatest need of our time is not economic, technological, social, political, or ecological. But this generation has again and again tried to solve our greatest problem through secular solutions. The greatest need of our generation is for the church to be the church. Through the powerful, spiritual, and moral influence of dynamic churches, these contemporary problems would be resolved."[47]

14.E. PLANNING FOR CHURCH EVANGELISM

Making plans can be a very spiritual activity. While being spontaneous may seem spiritual, it must be remembered that God the Holy Spirit can lead you a week or a month in advance as well as He can inspire you ten minutes in advance. Pray and plan and trust the Holy Spirit to do more than you ever imagined.

14.E.1. DAYTON-FRASER PLANNING MODEL

An evangelism strategy should result in a Great Commission plan. How is your congregation fulfilling its biblical mandates? What is your plan? Almost any plan will do, but have a plan and execute it. An excellent example of a planning model comes from the book *Planning Strategies for World Evangelization* by Edward R. Dayton and David A. Fraser. Their approach is as follows:

Step One: Define the Mission (purpose of ministry or event)

Step Two: Describe the People You Are Trying to Reach (demographics, worldview)

Step Three: Describe the Force for Evangelism (number of workers, level of training)

Step Four: Examine Means and Methods (research effective methods)

Step Five: Define and Approach (what are you going to do?)

Step Six: Anticipate Outcomes (prepare for growth, does this fit into your strategy?)

Step Seven: Decide Our Role (how much will you delegate?)

Step Eight: Make Plans (remember, all plans will need adaptation)

Step Nine: Act

Step Ten: Evaluate (measurable goals will assist in planning future successes)[48]

14.E.2 EVENT EVANGELISM PLANNING MODEL

Revivals, block parties, and other evangelistic events can be a way of reaching the lost and the unchurched. Each type of evangelistic event can be used effectively in its proper context. Whatever event a church decides to use, they should invest significant time in planning.

Describe the event:

1. Who is the target audience of the event?

2. What are the outcomes we expect from the event?

    2.1 What evangelism training will be needed?

    2.2 What leadership training will be needed? How will we recruit leaders?

    2.3 What measurable goals will help us to evaluate this event? (gospel presentations)

3. Where will the event be held? Neutral site or at the church?

4. When is the best time for the event?

5. What follow up will be made for new decisions for Christ at this event?

Special arrangements: If you schedule outside speakers or other special guests, then you should plan on how to take care of their expenses and needs. Churches often struggle on what to pay a speaker or group and how to plan for their accommodations. Some speakers have an agency, and their agency may dictate what their requirements are. Some speakers or groups will come on a love offering basis. As the host, if you take a love offering and advertise that the offering is for the revival team or group, then all of the receipts should go to the team and reasonable expenses should be paid in addition to that. A church can budget for this in its planning cycle.

Always be clear with the team about their daily expectations, and find out if they have any special dietary needs or other requirements. Clear and detailed communication on the front end will save wounded feelings on the back end. If you do not know the evangelist, speaker, or team ahead of time, do research and make sure that they are a good fit for your ministry situation.

Special events that are not revivals can still use many of the same principles outlined above. A good idea is to treat guests who have come to minister to you with honor and generosity. If you teach your congregation to honor people in ministry, they will learn to honor you and your ministry as well.

14.E.3. DISCIPLESHIP AS A PLAN FOR EVANGELISM

Discipleship can be used as a plan for evangelism. Whether a church uses the phrase, "Sunday school," or something else, the basic principles remain the same. The best discipleship programs teach believers to share their faith and then bring converts (or even seekers if the format allows for it) into discipleship groups and continue to reproduce.

Although the works are from the last century, philosophically two books still have much practical advice for churches today. L. R. Scarborough's *With Christ After the Lost* included a chapter entitled, "The Soul-Winning Sunday School."[49] Also, Arthur Flake's *Building a Standard Sunday School* is a second work with several timeless principles. What became known as Flake's Formula contained the following principles that will still work in a congregation today:

1. Discover the prospects

2. Expand the organization

3. Train the workers

4. Provide the space

5. Go after the people[50]

Whatever discipleship method a church uses, the main principles should be the following:

1. Intentional evangelism: looking for witnessing opportunities

2. Small group discipleship: built around the Scriptures

3. Evangelism should feed into discipleship

4. Discipleship should feed into evangelism

14.E.4 EVANGELISM OUTREACH STRATEGY: DEVELOPING PROSPECTS FOR YOUR CHURCH

The following section on evangelism outreach strategy and developing prospects comes from a series of interviews by the editor with Thomas Hammond, Executive Director of the Georgia Baptist Convention.

Effective local church evangelism requires a biblical, balanced approach. It is possible that over fifty percent of Southern Baptist churches have no intentional evangelism plan or program. Proverbs 29:18 (NASB) states, "Where there is no vision, the people are unrestrained, But happy is he who keeps the law." If over ninety percent of Southern Baptists were to die without sharing their faith, what does that say about the vision of our churches? A careful plan is needed that leads with vision and is practical enough to be understood and implemented by the local church and the average believer.

An example of how a vision and strategy can be constructed would look like this:

The Elements of an Evangelism Strategy

1. Prayer Evangelism—pray for the lost in an organized manner

2. Personal Evangelism—the leader must do it themselves first!

3. Ministry Evangelism—disciple the flock to do evangelism

4. Visitation/Follow Up—go to the harvest field

5. Leadership Development—train the trainers

Once a vision and strategy are in place, you can begin to develop methods to assist church members in the discipline of evangelism. A reminder such as a "3:16" (for John 3:16) card can be kept with your phone or in your wallet. The card would state, "Six days per week, pray for three lost people for one hour." One company advertises by asking what is in your wallet; in this case the question is, "Who is in your wallet?" Mid-America Baptist Theological Seminary has a Witness 1:7 program. Each student must share the gospel once every seven days to receive credit for the academic work in that semester. This program is intended to build a disciplined habit of sharing the gospel weekly into the life of every minister of the gospel.

Prayer in evangelism must be focused on the lost. Many times, prayer focuses on physical needs to the point that we spend more time praying to keep people out of heaven than to get them into heaven. Prayer should focus on seeing people come to Christ and then following the Lord in believer's baptism. A quick guide would be to: Pray, Serve, Tell. You can prayer walk your neighborhoods. You can pray for city employees by name for a year. Pray that God will give you favor with the lost people of the community. Let your prayer drive you to serve others in the community and this will open doors to tell lost people the gospel. Develop the discipline to commit to an eight-week prayer strategy to "pray your neighbors to Christ."

As churches seek to expand their Great Commission outreach, they should take concrete steps to ensure that this happens. Examples of key steps would include the following:

1. Set up a visitation plan. You need a comprehensive plan from visitor card to visit. Remember that you are going to make a friend not just make a visit. Make sure that in the connecting process someone asks the prospect if they have a personal relationship with Christ. Develop creative ways to capture visitor information. Many churches will mention that visitor information cards are available but then take the

offering before the prospect even had time to fill out the card. Test your visitor information collection process to see if it works!

2. Take your Vacation Bible School and make it a Great Commission event (not just church daycare).

3. Develop a spirit of receptivity on your campus to guests. Do not assume your church is visitor friendly, investigate for yourself! What does a visitor experience in their first ten minutes on your campus? Most churches are structured to welcome church attenders but never give thought to receiving guests who have never been to a church before. Two "Rs" that bring us back every Sunday: relationship (vertical and horizontal) and responsibility. Assume someone has never been to a church before. In other words, start thinking like a cross-cultural missionary. Where visitors are concerned, assume nothing, explain everything. Develop a measuring gage that will let you know how you are doing in visitation and membership retention. Creatively invest the time in a plan to assimilate and involve people.

4. Have a celebratory worship service. Combine majesty and joy in every event.

5. Establish ministry in your church that is not for the church. Be outwardly focused. For example, give members a list of forty different areas where they could serve. In Matthew 13 Jesus gives the parable of the seed and the sower. How do the four types of soil inform your planning? How can you reach people in different life situations?

Finally, you should decide how you can motivate and mentor people in doing evangelism. Questions you should be asking are the following:

1. What does the pastor want to accomplish in evangelism training?

2. How does the church integrate evangelism training and follow-up into the life of the church?

3. What mentor training materials are needed?

4. Can we produce evangelism and discipleship materials ourselves?

5. How can we discover prospects for evangelism?

Your church can develop your own toolkit with the following items:

1. Introduction to Evangelism. "Welcome to Great Commission Now."

2. Leader Guide for the pastor and staff. This should focus on strategy.

3. Mentor Handbook. How can a trainer train a person to witness?

4. Apprentice Manual. The material a new witness for Christ needs to know.

5. Supporting materials. An example would be gospel tracts. Also, information on lostness can be beneficial. Sites with helpful information such as *Statistical Atlas* can be used.[51]

The goal of a local, New Testament church is to saturate the community with the gospel, win people to Christ, take the gospel to the nations, plant new churches, and repeat until the return of the Lord Jesus.

Maintaining a database of prospects is a key in any effective evangelism strategy. Finding new members of the community (real estate agents know who they are!) and asking current members and attenders to identify prospects, are just two ways to identify prospects. Identifying people's needs and providing care for those needs can also enhance a church's outreach.

Sample Evangelistic Strategy Checklist

1. Prayer Ministry—An active, organized prayer team needs to be in place to ask the Lord: to call out workers for evangelism and full-time ministry and missions; to pray for lost prospects to receive the gospel; and to pray for new converts as they begin their journey with Christ.

2. Church Evangelism Strategy—Three-year vision and mission plan; remember the goal is always the world. You should choose a discipleship program and choose or develop an evangelism training approach that moves from Level 1 evangelism to Level 3 evangelism. Remember you may need to keep Level 1 training each year even as you add higher levels of training.

May God bless you as you follow through and witness to other people.
—B. Gray Allison

APPENDIX 1:
PERSONAL EVANGELISM MEMORY VERSE LIST

Week 1
John 3:3
Acts 16:31
Romans 14:12

Week 2
Isaiah 53:6
Isaiah 59:2
Jeremiah 17:9

Week 3
Romans 3:10
Romans 3:23
Matthew 6:33

Week 4
Romans 6:23
Matthew 7:21
John 5:24

Week 5
Romans 5:8
Romans 10:9
Romans 10:10

Week 6
Romans 10:11
Romans 10:13
Romans 6

Week 7
Acts 20:20
Acts 20:21
Acts 20:32

Week 8
John 1:12
John 3:18
2 Corinthians 5:21

Week 9
Revelation 3:20
Revelation 21:8
Revelation 22:17

Week 10
John 10:28
John 14:15
Ecclesiastes 7:20

Week 11
Matthew 10:32
Matthew 10:33
Acts 4:12

Week 12
Luke 6:46
John 14:21
John 14:23

Week 13
1 John 2:4
James 4:17
1 Peter 2:24

Week 14
Matthew 11:28
Matthew 12:30
Luke 13:3

Week 15
1 John 1:8
1 John 1:9
1 John 1:10

Week 16
Acts 10:43
Acts 13:39
Galatians 2:21

Week 17
Acts 2:38
Acts 2:41
Acts 2:47

Week 18
John 6:44
Proverbs 20:9
Proverbs 29:1

Week 19
2 Corinthians 5:19
2 Corinthians 6:2
2 Peter 3:9

Week 20
1 Peter 1:18
1 Peter 1:19
Titus 3:5

Week 21
John 3:36
Hebrews 7:25
Hebrews 10:25

Week 22
1 John 3:4
James 1:15
Ezekiel 18:4

Week 23
Ephesians 2:8
Ephesians 2:9
Ephesians 2:10

Week 24
Matthew 9:12
Mark 10:18
Romans 2:5

Week 25
Isaiah 1:18
Isaiah 55:6
Isaiah 55:7

Week 26
Romans 12:1
Romans 12:2
Luke 19:10

APPENDIX 2:
ALLISON ANNOTATED BIBLIOGRAPHY

This annotated bibliography originally appeared as B. Gray Allison, "Annotated Bibliography," *Baptist Training Union Magazine* 8 (620) October 1965.

There are many helpful books for church members that are concerned with evangelism. Some deal with motivation, some with method, and some with a combination of the two. An attempt is made in the following bibliography to balance these two approaches.

1. C.E. Autrey, *You Can Win Souls*

Dr. Autrey needs no introduction to Southern Baptists. He is director of the Division of Evangelism of the Home Mission Board, Southern Baptist Convention. In this book, Dr. Autrey deals with basic things to know and do in effective witnessing. This is a fine "how to" book which any layman can use with profit.

2. Theron Chastain, *We Can Win Others*

The basic outline of this book shows its worth: "How the Early Christian Won Others"; "The Biblical Basis for Evangelism"; "The Evangelistic Church"; "Plans for Action"; "Methods That Win"; "Personal Growth and Development." Chapters 4 and 5 are especially good for the lay witness.

3. Gene Edwards, *Here's How to Win Souls*

This brief work is a "how to" book. It deals step by step with the technique of personal witnessing. It tells how to enter the home, how to engage in conversation with the lost person, how to present the plan of salvation, and how to draw the net. This book will be of great assistance to any witness for Christ.

4. Eugene Myers Harrison, *How to Win Souls*

This book by the professor of missions and evangelism at Wheaton College is one of the best I have seen on personal evangelism. Harrison's book is practical in motivating witnesses and instructing them in methods.

5. Roland Q. Leavell, *Evangelism: Christ's Imperative Commission*

This is one of the most outstanding books on total evangelism that I have ever read. Dr. Leavell devotes Part I to motivation and Part II to a history of evangelism. Parts III and IV are concerned with methods and techniques in church evangelism and personal evangelism which will help any Christian witness. The suggestions that he makes are down to earth and can be easily followed.

6. J.C. Macauley and Robert H. Belton, *Personal Evangelism*

This is an excellent work on personal witnessing by the president of London College of the Bible and missions and the instructor in evangelism and Bible at Moody Bible Institute. The section dealing with motivation to witness and the suggestions on the actual witnessing are good and very helpful.

7. Stephen F. Olford, *Successful Soul-Winning*

The pastor of Calvary Baptist Church in New York is described by Billy Graham as "one of the most successful soul winners I have ever met." Dr. Olford writes of the task, training, technique, target, travail, trials, temptations, and triumph of the soul winner. This is an excellent "how to" book.

8. L.R. Scarborough, *With Christ After the Lost*

This is a most practical book on witnessing. Parts IV and V, dealing with "Personal Work" and "Scripture Passages for Workers," are excellent aids for those who would be effective in witnessing for Christ.

9. Samuel M. Shoemaker, *Revive Thy Church Beginning with Me*

Two brief quotes from this book by the late rector of Calvary Church, Pittsburg, will show why it was selected for this bibliography: "Until something happens *to* us and *in* us, it will not happen *through* us." "Shall we remain content with our present spiritual powerlessness . . . or shall we let a divine discontent come into our hearts, shall we pray and wrestle till we are blessed and changed? Shall we ask God to take us over completely, and in spite of all our known weakness and inexperience to use us in human lives and situations? He has the power to give us if we will take it. Shall we ask for it—and take the consequences?"

10. Elton Trueblood, *Your Other Vocation*

This little volume is concerned with getting laymen involved in the major task of the churches: that of evangelism. It is basically a "why" book, but it gives helpful suggestions for the outreach of laymen.

APPENDIX 3:
B. GRAY ALLISON ADDRESS TO THE 1989 SOUTHERN BAPTIST CONVENTION

(from the archives of the Southern Baptist Historical Society, Nashville, TN)

THEME INTERPRETATION, 1989 SBC MEETING, LAS VEGAS, NV

For release after 9:25 AM, Tuesday, June 13, 1989

B. Gray Allison is president and professor of evangelism of Mid-America Baptist Theological Seminary, Memphis, Tenn. Before coming to that position in 1972, he was pastor in his native state of Louisiana; served on the faculty of New Orleans Baptist Theological Seminary, New Orleans; was associate director of evangelism for the home mission board, Atlanta, Ga.; and was a vocational evangelist. He is a graduate of Louisiana Tech University, Ruston, La., and New Orleans Baptist Theological Seminary. He and his wife, the former Voncille Cruse, have three children.

"Going, Weeping, Sowing, Reaping"
Jude 20–23
By B. Gray Allison

The President of the Convention notified me that he had staked out the theme from Psalm 126 for his Presidential Address. Therefore, I have turned to another passage to deal with our theme of "Going, Weeping, Sowing, Reaping."

I call to your attention Jude, verses 20 through 23. "But ye, beloved, building up yourselves on your most holy faith, praying in the Holy Ghost, Keep yourselves in the love of God, looking for the mercy of our Lord Jesus Christ unto eternal life. And of some have compassion, making a difference: And others save with fear, pulling them out of the fire; hating even the garment spotted by the flesh." Our major task is to win others to Christ.

Our theme for this convention is "Going, Weeping, Sowing, Reaping." If we are to be witnesses, there are some prerequisites.

I. THE PREREQUISITES FOR THE WITNESS

A. "Building Up Yourselves on Your Most Holy Faith"

The thing which appalls me as I go from church to church in our Southern Baptist Convention is the abysmal ignorance of the Word of God on the part of God's people. Most of our folks do not know what God has said. We talk a lot about the Bible, but we do not study it. If we are to be the witnesses we should be, we must saturate ourselves with the Word of God. This is what Jude was talking about when he said, "Building up yourselves on your most holy faith."

Our faith is a holy faith. This means that it is a different, a set-apart, a separate faith. It is not man-made. It is God-given. It is not commitment to a hierarchy. It is not even commitment to a Book, but it is commitment to a Person—Jesus Christ, the Son of God.

How does one build himself up on this holy faith? It is by studying the Word of God. Paul said to the elders of Ephesus, "I commend you to God, and to the word of his grace, which is able to build you up" (Acts 20:32). Peter said, "As newborn babes, desire the sincere milk of the word, that ye may grow thereby" (1 Peter 2:2). We must study the Word of God. There is no substitute for regular, daily, personal study of the Word of God if we are to be effective in our witness.

I was discussing this in a church one evening. After the service a young mother came to me. She had three small children. She was weeping. She said, "Brother Allison, you just don't understand. I don't have time to study the Bible. You are not a mother. You wouldn't understand that."

I said, "No ma'am, I am not a mother. I never will be, but I had one. My mother did not rear three children. She reared nine children. She did this in the days when we had no conveniences in our home. We did not have running water and for many years did not even have electricity. She sewed for four girls, patched for five boys, darned socks, gardened, kept the house, cooked, walked over the hills of north Louisiana selling magazine subscriptions so that she could buy good reading material for her children, and walked those hills selling "Fashion Frocks" so that she could help my father feed, clothe, and educate nine children. She was the best witness for her opportunity that I have known. She wore out Bible after Bible in her personal study of the Word of God. When she died, each one of the nine received at least one of her worn out Bibles."

Many times we say that we do not have time. But, we do what we want to do. If we are to be effective in our witness, we must build up ourselves on our most holy faith.

B. "Praying in the Holy Ghost"

Now, this does not mean what some of my friends think that it means. They think that this means praying in an unknown tongue. It has nothing to do with an unknown tongue. It simply means—praying led by the Holy Spirit of God. We do not have many people today who will really pray; but, if we are to be effective in our witness, we must pray. If we pray led by the Holy Spirit, we will not be selfish in our praying. We will thank God more; we will praise Him more; and we will pray more earnestly and fervently for others. How long has it been since you got on your knees and cried out in prayer to God in Heaven for someone who is lost? Our crying need for this day is people who know the Word of God and who are people of prayer. We need folks who will pray as the apostle Paul did when he said, "I could wish that myself were accursed from Christ for my brethren, my kinsmen according to the flesh" (Romans 9:3).

We need people who will pray like John Knox prayed when he said, "Give me Scotland or I die." We need people who will pray like Hudson Taylor did when he said, "God, something must be done for inland China or I die." We desperately need *prayer warriors* in our day!

C. "Keep Yourselves in the Love of God"

This does not mean to go around mumbling, "God loves me. God loves me. God loves me." I have some friends who do this, and it drives me nuts! It does not mean running around saying, "I love God. I love God. I love God." That will drive you crazy also. There are times when you need to stand up in public and say, "I love the Lord." That is not what Jude is talking about here.

Jude is talking about staying in the Will of God for one's life. Find the center of God's Will, get in it, and stay there. If we are to be effective in our witness, we are going to have to get right with God, stay right with God, and keep in the Will of God, so that He can shower His love and grace upon us. Then our lives will be beautiful and holy and will draw others to our wonderful Savior.

II. "LOOKING FOR THE MERCY OF OUR LORD JESUS CHRIST UNTO ETERNAL LIFE"

Surely Jude is talking about the return of our blessed Lord. "Looking for the mercy of our Lord Jesus Christ unto eternal life." I do not really understand eternal life, but I have it. I certainly do not understand God's mercy, but I have experienced it. I also am looking for the coming of our

Savior. The word translated "looking" does not mean idly gazing around saying, "Maybe Jesus will come today." It is the same form as in Titus 2:13. It is a word which means "expectant longing." Can you imagine what would happen if all of us seated in this hall today who claim to know Jesus Christ as Lord were truly expecting Him to return today, longing for Him to come today? It would change our world and His people if we really believed, really expected, really longed for Him to come.

My mother had three sons in the service during the Second World War. All three of us were overseas when the war ended. All three of us had enough points to get out. (Some of you will remember the point system in the Second World War.)

I was on the little island of Ie Shima, right off Okinawa, when the war ended. On the third of November 1945, my C.O. called me in and said, "Allison, would you like to fly your own plane home?" I said, "Yes, sir, indeed I would." He said, "Get your crew together. The orders will be cut and you can leave today." We flew to Manila in the Philippines and spent the night. We flew from there to Tinian and spent a night and on across the Pacific to Mather Field in Sacramento, California. Then, I flew down to Barksdale Field in Shreveport, Louisiana, got a three-day pass, got on a bus, and rode 37 miles north to my hometown of Ida, Louisiana.

I had not written my mother; I had not called her; I had not cabled her. She thought I was 8,000 miles away across the ocean. The dear bus driver was kind enough to let me out in front of Mama's house. I walked into the house, thinking that I would surprise her; but I really didn't. You see, every day since VJ Day, she had expected her boys to come home. She longed for us to come home; and, in her expectant longing for us to come, she was prepared for our coming. There were fresh sheets on my bed, and fresh flowers in the vase on the nightstand by my bed in the middle of November in north Louisiana. There were fresh cookies and a fresh cake baked in the kitchen in those days of sugar rationing. I don't know how she did it; but every three or four days, she would bake a fresh batch of cookies. Her boys were coming home.

My dear people, if we truly expected Jesus, if we longed for Him to come, it would make us ready for Him to come. That means we would be in His Will for our lives; and that means that we would be faithful in our witness to draw others to know Him, so that they, too, would be prepared for His coming.

III. THE PERSONS OF THE WITNESS

Who are those to whom we are to witness? Jude gives us three groups.

A. "Of Some Have Compassion, Making a Difference"

There are some who just need to be "suffered along with." That is, they need to be handled carefully and lovingly. There are children growing up in Christian homes, growing up in churches. They are not bitter toward God, they are not mean and ugly, but they are sinners. They need somebody to explain to them what sin is and what sin does. They need someone to tell them what God has done for us in Jesus and tell them the claims of Jesus on their lives and draw them to Him.

I shall never forget the night when my Charlotte (then 7½ years old) went with me to a place where I was to preach. On our way home that evening, she said, "Daddy, I should have come forward at the invitation tonight." I said, "Why, sweetheart?" She said, "Daddy, I am lost; and I need to be saved." I pulled off on the side of the road, turned on the dome light, took out my little New Testament, and talked with her about her sin, her need of a Savior, and the claims of Jesus Christ in her life. She gave her life to Jesus that night in that car on the side of the road and has lived a consistent Christian life for Him now for more than 26 years.

B. "Others Save with Fear, Pulling Them Out of the Fire"

There are some people who, because of age or illness, even if our Savior delays His coming, are on the very verge of eternity. These are people who have had opportunity after opportunity and have not responded to the love of God. We need to go to them with a holy boldness and, as it were, pull them back out of the very fires of Hell itself. We can't wait. We must go with boldness.

I remember so well a dear friend who was much older than I. He was from my hometown and had left, when he was a young boy, to work in the oil fields. He did well, invested his money, and prospered. When he was in his late fifties, he returned to Ida and retired. For a period of about 25 years, I witnessed to him consistently. When I would go home to see my mother, I would go by to see him and witness to him. Many times, he wept as I shared with him about Christ, but he always said, "I just can't do that now, Gray."

I was in a Bible Conference in Shreveport, Louisiana, and decided that I would go up and spend the night with my brother in Ida. The next morning, I decided that I would go by and see my friend before I went back to Shreveport. I went to his home and drank coffee with him and his wife. I shared with him again about God's love and Jesus and the claim of Christ on his life. Again, tears came to his eyes; but he said, "I just can't do that now, Gray." I pressed the claims of Christ on him, but he said, "I can't do that now."

I had always asked him if I could pray for him before I left his home, and I asked again. He assented. I began to pray for him, and as I prayed a conviction came to my heart. l did something I have never done before or since. In the middle of my prayer, I stopped and said, "Ben, I want you to pray. I want you to repeat after me anything I say that you can really mean in your heart." Then I prayed, "Dear God." He didn't say anything. I said, "Ben, anybody can say, "Dear God." He said, "Dear God." Then, I led him in a sinner's prayer; and he repeated it sentence by sentence. I looked up and said, "Ben, did you mean what you just said?" He said, "I really did." I said, "Ben, if you meant what you prayed to God, then God has saved you." He said, "That's right." I said, "Well, Ben, what do you do when somebody gives you a gift?" He said, "I thank them." I said, "Wouldn't you like to thank God? He has just given you the most wonderful gift in the world—eternal life in Jesus." He said, "I certainly would," and bowed his head and thanked God for saving him. I asked Ben to get his Bible; and he said, "I don't have one, but I will get my wife's." He brought it to me, and I wrote in there what he had just done; and I said, "Ben, is this what you did?" And he said, "Yes." I said, "Will you sign your name?" He said, "I certainly will." And he did. l wrote under it: John 3:16. I said, "Ben, your children and grandchildren will pick up this Bible and read this and rejoice and rejoice and rejoice." I asked him to join the church with his wife. She was a Methodist. She had served the Lord faithfully all those years. He did. I preached in my little home church on Easter Sunday after that, and they came to hear me. He said, "Gray, we have been married 60 years, but our life is so much more wonderful now."

Ben died not too long after that, and I had a sweet letter from his wife telling me how he loved the Lord and how he talked about Him and how glad she was he was in Heaven. Sometimes, we must go with a holy boldness to people to draw them to Jesus.

C. "Hating Even the Garment Spotted by the Flesh"

Are we to go to the gamblers, the dope addicts, the drunkards, the prostitutes, the openly wicked and vicious people in this world? Indeed, we are. Jesus did, and we must do it also. But, Jude is saying that we need to be careful how we go, where we go, and when we go. A cardinal rule—never go alone to visit a person who is living in open sin. Be careful where you go; be careful when you go; but, dear friend, do go. Jesus did; and we must, too.

I went with a pastor in Pennsylvania some years ago to visit a woman. She was living openly with a man who was not her husband. They were drinking, cursing, living in terrible sin. We knocked on the door of the apartment, and she came to the door. The robe she had on was dirty, and it smelled of vomit and wine. Her hair was matted. Her face mottled. Her eyes were red. She invited us in. There were old magazines, newspapers, whiskey bottles, beer bottles, and cigarette butts on the floor.

There, in the midst of all of that filth, I talked with that lady about our Lord and His love for her. She didn't believe that He could love someone like her. I told her the story of the woman at the well in Samaria and how Jesus saved her. That woman got down on her knees in the midst of that filth and prayed, confessing her sins to God, asking His forgiveness, and inviting Jesus into her life. She got up from her knees with the most radiant glow on her face that I think I have seen. What a marvelous transformation in the face of that woman. Folks, we must go. We must go.

Would you care if someone you had met day by day,
Should Never be told about Jesus?
Would you care if he, in the judgement, should say,
"No one ever told me about Jesus."
—Author Unknown

You see, wherever you are, He has put you there. You say,

"Master, where shall I work today?"
And my love flowed warm and free.
Then he pointed out a tiny plot,
And said, "Work there for me."
But I answered quickly, "Oh no, not there,
Why, no one would ever see,
No matter how well my work was done,
Not that small place for me."
His voice when he answered was not stern;
He answered me tenderly,
"Disciple, search that heart of thine:
Are you working for them or Me?
Nazareth was just a little place,
And so was Galilee."
—Author Unknown

You see, wherever you are, wherever He has put you,

He is counting on you,
On a love that will share
In His burden of prayer
For those He has bought
With His lifeblood, and sought
Through His sorrow and pain
To win home again.
He is counting on you.
If you fail Him,
What then?
—Author Unknown

APPENDIX 4:
SELECTED POEMS BY B. GRAY ALLISON

GOING HOME TO HEAVEN

I'm going home to Heaven
Where my Savior waits for me.
He prepared me for the journey
Through His death on Calvary.

I'm going home to Heaven
Where my loved ones wait for me.
For they too have shared the blessings
Which are in His victory.

I'm going home to Heaven
There to live eternally.
For the life of Christ my Savior
Is the life He gave to me.

I'm going home to Heaven
Won't you come and go with me?
Jesus who died and rose again
Is waiting there for me.
—B.G.A.

COMFORT

In the hour of the dawning
When the sun begins to shine,
I can hear the Master saying,
"Fear not, you are always mine."

In the heat of the noon-day
With the burdens it can bring,
I can hear the Master saying,
"Fear not, I am still the King."

In the hour of the twilight,
When the dark begins to come,
I can hear the Master saying,
"Fear not, I've prepared a home."

In the still of the midnight
When the darkest hours come,
I can hear the Master saying,
"Fear not, I will bring you home."

So I come to Him rejoicing
And I speak to Him in prayer
I can hear the Master saying,
"Leave with me your every care."
—B.G.A., May 31, 1998

THE WORD NOT SPOKEN

I thought at the close of day
Of the word not spoken,
To those I met on the way
Whose very hearts were broken.

I thought of the man I'd met
Whose spirit was crushed, broken,
And my heart beat in me sore
For the word not spoken.

I thought of the friend who's lost,
Whose very soul is broken,
And my conscience still condemns me
For the word not spoken.
—B.G.A., July 23, 1991

APPENDIX 5:
SELECTED BIBLIOGRAPHY

Adcock, E., *Charles H. Spurgeon*. Anderson, IN: Gospel Trumpet Company, 1925.

Akins, Thomas Wade. *Pioneer Evangelism: Growing Churches and Planting New Ones that Are Self-Supporting Using New Testament Methods*. Rio de Janeiro, Brazil: Home Mission Board of the Brazilian Baptist Convention, 1995.

Akins, Wade. *Sharing Your Faith with Muslims*. Garland, TX: Hannibal Books, 2011.

Albus, H. J. *The Boy from Northfield*. Grand Rapids: Wm. B. Eerdmans Publishing Company, 1950.

Aldrich, Joseph. *Life-Style Evangelism*. Portland, OR: Multnomah, 1981.

Allison, B. Gray. "Annotated Bibliography," *Baptist Training Union Magazine* 8 (620), October 1965.

Allison, B. Gray. "Issues in Evangelism." In *Mid-America Theological Journal*. Vol. 22, 1998.

Allison, B. Gray. "Person to Person." In *Royal Service Magazine*. Vol. 60, No. 7. Birmingham: Woman's Missionary Union of the Southern Baptist Convention, 1966.

Archibald, A. C. *New Testament Evangelism—How It Works Today*. Philadelphia: The Judson Press, 1947.

Arn, Win and Charles Arn. *The Master's Plan for Making Disciples: How Every Christian Can Be an Effective Witness Through an Enabling Church*. Monrovia, CA: Church Growth, 1982.

Augsburger, Myron, Calvin C. Ratz, and Frank Tillapaugh. *Mastering Outreach and Evangelism*. Washington: Christianity Today Multnomah, 1990.

Autrey, C. E. *Basic Evangelism*. Grand Rapids: Zondervan, 1959.

Autrey, C. E. *Evangelism in the Acts*. Grand Rapids: Zondervan, 1964.

Autrey, C. E. *You Can Win Souls*. Nashville: Broadman, 1961.

Bader, Jesse M. *Evangelism in a Changing America*. St. Louis: Bethany Press, 1957.

Baker, Gordon Pratt. *A Practical Theology for Christian Evangelism*. Nashville: Graded Press, 1965.

Banks, Louis Albert. *Sermons Which Have Won Souls*. New York: Funk & Wagnalls Company, 1908.

Barna, George. *Evangelism that Works: How to Reach Changing Generations with the Unchanging Gospel*. Ventura, CA: Regel, 1995.

Bauckham, Richard, ed. *The Gospel for All Christians: Rethinking the Gospel Audiences*. Grand Rapids: Wm. B. Eerdmans Publishing Company, 1998.

Belden, Albert D. *George Whitefield*. London: Rockcliff, 1953.

Biederwolf, William E. *Evangelism: Its Justification, Its Operation and Its Value*. London: Fleming H. Revell Company, 1921.

Bonar, Horatius. *Words to Winners of Souls*. Revised ed. New York: American Tract Society, 1950.

Brawner, Jeff. *How to Share Christ with Your Friends of Another Faith*. Garland, TX: Hannibal Books, 2012.

Bright, Bill. *Witnessing Without Fear*. San Bernardino, CA: Here's Life Publishers, 1987.

Brock, Charles. *I Have Been Born Again, What Next?* Neosho, MO: Church Growth International, n.d.

Brooks, E. P. *The Real Billy Sunday*. Dayton, OH: Otterbein Press, 1914.

Bryan, Dawson C. *A Handbook of Evangelism for Laymen*. Nashville: Abingdon-Cokesbury Press, 1948.

Broughton, Len G. *The Soul-Winning Church*. London: Fleming H. Revell Company, 1905.

Burroughs, P. E. *Winning to Christ: A Study in Evangelism*. Nashville: Sunday School Board of the Southern Baptist Convention Publishers, 1923.

Cahill, Mark. *One Thing You Can't Do in Heaven*. Rockwall, TX: Biblical Discipleship Publishers, 2010.

Cameron, Kirk and Ray Comfort. *The Way of the Master: How to Share Your Faith Simply, Effectively, Biblically . . . the Way Jesus Did*. Wheaton: Tyndale House   Publishers, Inc., 2004.

Carson, D. A. *Christ & Culture Revisited*. Grand Rapids: Eerdmans, 2008.

Casaldo, Chris. *Talking with Catholics About the Gospel*. Grand Rapids: Zondervan, 2015.

Chafin, Kenneth. *Help, I'm a Layman*. Waco: Word Books, 1966.

Chastain, Theron. *We Can Win Others*. Philadelphia: The Judson Press, 1953.

Chester, Tim. *A Meal With Jesus*. Wheaton: Crossway, 2011.

Coleman, Robert. *The Great Commission Lifestyle*. Wilmore, KY: Department of Evangelism, Asbury Theological Seminary, 1963.

Coleman, Robert. *The Heart of the Gospel*. Grand Rapids: Baker, 2011.

Coleman, Robert E. *The Master Plan of Evangelism: 30th Anniversary Edition*. Foreword by Billy Graham. Grand Rapids: Fleming H. Revell, 1993.

Coleman, Robert E. *The Master's Way of Personal Evangelism*. Wheaton: Crossway Books, 1997.

Conant, J. E. *Every-Member Evangelism*. Introduction by J. C. Massee. New York: Harper & Brothers Publishers, 1922.

Conant, J. E. *Soul-Winning Evangelism*. Grand Rapids: Zondervan, 1963.

Conwell, Russel. *Life of Charles Haddon Spurgeon*. Philadelphia: Edgewood Publishing Company, 1892.

Crockett, William V. and James G. Sigountos, eds. *Through No Fault of Their Own? The Fate of Those Who Have Never Heard*. Preface by Kenneth S. Kantzer. Grand Rapids: Baker Book House, 1991.

Crouch, Austin. *The Plan of Salvation and How to Teach It*. Nashville: Sunday School Board of the Southern Baptist Convention, 1924.

Curtis, Richard K. *They Called Him Mr. Moody*. Grand Rapids: Eerdmans, 1967.

Dana, Harvey E. *Lee Rutland Scarborough: A Life of Service*. Nashville: Broadman Press, 1942.

Dawson, Scott, ed. *The Complete Evangelism Guidebook*. Grand Rapids: Baker, 2006.

Day, Richard E. *Man of Like Passions*. Grand Rapids: Zondervan, 1942.

Day, Richard E. *The Shadow of the Broad Brim*. Philadelphia: The Judson Press, 1934.

Dayton, Edward K. and David A Fraser. *Planning Strategies for World Evangelization*. Grand Rapids: Eerdmans, 1990.

Dobbins, Gaines S. *Evangelism According to Christ*. Nashville: Broadman Press, 1945.

Downey, Murray W. *The Art of Soul-Winning*. Grand Rapids: Baker, 1957.

Drier, Mary Sue Dehmlow, ed. *Created and Led by the Spirit*. Grand Rapids: Eerdmans, 2013.

Drummond, Lewis. *The Evangelist*. Nashville: Word Publishing, 2001.

Drummond, Lewis. *Reaching Generation Next*. Grand Rapids: Baker, 2002.

Drummond, Lewis A. *The Word of the Cross: A Contemporary Theology of Evangelism*. Foreword by J. I. Packer. Nashville: Broadman Press, 1992.

Edman, V. *Finney Lives On*. New York: Fleming H. Revell Company, 1951.

Edwards, Gene. *Here's How to Win Souls*. Tyler, TX: Soul Winning Publications, 1960.

Eisenman, Tom L. *Everyday Evangelism: Making the Most of Life's Common Moments: With Study Questions for Individuals or Groups*. Downers Grove, IL: InterVarsity Press, 1987.

Ellis, H. W. *Fishing for Men: Including A Suggested Scheme of Organization for Bands of "Fishermen" together with a Plan and Program for Winning Those Who Are Lost and for Enlisting the Unenlisted Saved in the Service of Christ*. Grand Rapids: Zondervan Publishing House, 1941.

Ellis, James J. *Charles Haddon Spurgeon*. London: J. Nisbet and Company, 1891.

Ellis, William. *Billy Sunday, the Man and His Message*. Philadelphia: John C. Winston Company, 1936.

Exum, Jack H. *How to Win Souls Today*. Old Tappan, NJ: Revell, 1970.

Feather, R. Othal. *A Manual for Promoting Personal Evangelism Through the Sunday School*. Nashville: Convention Press, 1959.

Fields, Doug and Brett Eastman. *Sharing Jesus*. Grand Rapids: Zondervan, 2006.

Finney, Charles G. *Finney's Life and Lectures*. Grand Rapids: Zondervan, 1956.

Fish, Roy. *When Heaven Touched Earth: The Awakening of 1858 and Its Effects on Baptists*. Foreword by Henry Blackaby. Edited by Mack Tomlinson. Azle, TX: Need of the Times Publishers, 1996.

Fisher, Fred. *Christianity is Personal*. Nashville: Broadman Press, 1951.

Fitt, A. *Moody Still Lives*. Chicago: Moody Press, 1936.

Floyd, Ronnie. *Our Last Great Hope: Awakening the Great Commission*. Nashville: Thomas Nelson, 2011.

Ford, Leighton. *The Christian Persuader*. New York: Harper and Row, 1966.

Fuller, David. *C. H. Spurgeon's Autobiography*. Grand Rapids: Zondervan Publishing House, 1963.

Gage, Freddie. *Go Tell: The Soul Winners Encyclopedia*. Euless, TX: The Freddie Gage Evangelistic Association, 1980.

Gartenhaus, Jacob. *Winning Jews to Jesus*. Grand Rapids: Zondervan Publishing House, 1963.

Geisler, Norman and David Geisler. *Conversation Evangelism*. Eugene, OR: Harvest House, 2009.

Gerstner, John. *Steps to Salvation*. Philadelphia: The Westminster Press, 1960.

Gillenson, Lewis. *Billy Graham, the Man and His Message*. Greenwich, CT: Fawcett Publications, 1954.

Gledston, James P. *George Whitefield, M.A., Field Preacher*. New York: American Tract Society, 1901.

Goodell, Charles L. *Cyclopedia of Evangelism: Including the Books Heralds of a Passion, What Are You Worth? Pastor and Evangelist*. New York: Harper & Brothers, Publishers, 1921.

Goodell, Charles L. *Heralds of Passion*. New York: Ray Long & Richard R. Smith, 1932.

Goodell, Charles L. *Pastoral and Personal Evangelism*. New York: Fleming H. Revell Company, 1907.

Goodspeed, Edgar J. *A Full History of the Wonderful Career of Moody and Sankey*. St. John, N.B.: W. E. Erskine and Company, 1900.

Graham, Billy. *A Biblical Standard for Evangelists*. Minneapolis: World Wide Publications, 1984.

Graham, Billy. *Just As I Am: The Autobiography of Billy Graham*. San Francisco: HarperSanFrancisco, 1997.

Greear, J. D. *Gospel: Recovering the Power that Made Christianity Revolutionary*. Nashville: B & H Publishing Group, 2011.

Green, Bryan. *The Practice of Evangelism*. New York: Scribner's, 1951.

Green, Michael. *Evangelism in the Early Church*. Grand Rapids: William B. Eerdmans Publishing Company, 1970.

Green, O. Olin. *Normal Evangelism*. Introduction by Byron H. DeMent. New York: Fleming H. Revell Company, 1910.

Greeson, Kevin. *The Camel: How Muslims Are Coming to Faith in Christ!* Arkadelphia, AR: WIGTake Resources, LLC, 2007.

Ham, Ken. *Creation Evangelism for the New Millennium*. Green Forest, AR: Master Books, Inc. 1999.

Hamilton, W. W. *A Bible Revival*. Nashville: Broadman Press, 1940.

Hamilton, William Wistar. *Wisdom in Soul Winning*. Nashville: Sunday School Board of the Southern Baptist Convention, 1929.

Hanks, Billie, Jr. *Everyday Evangelism*. Grand Rapids: Zondervan, 1984.

Hardy, E. *George Whitefield*. New York: American Tract Society, 1938.

Harrison, Eugene. *How to Win Souls*. Wheaton: Scripture Press, 1952.

Harrt, Julian N. *Toward a Theology of Evangelism*. Nashville: Abingdon Press, 1955.

Havlik, John F. *The Evangelistic Church*. Nashville: Convention Press, 1976.

Hawkins, O. S. *Drawing the Net: 30 Practical Principles for Leading Others to Christ Publicly and Personally*. N.p.: Annuity Board of the Southern Baptist Convention, 2002.

Head, E. E. *Evangelism in Acts*. Fort Smith, AR: Southwestern Baptist Theological Seminary, 1950.

Hemphill, Ken. *The Antioch Effect: 8 Characteristics of Highly Effective Churches*. Nashville: Broadman and Holman Publishers, 1994.

Hemphill, Ken and R. Wayne Jones. *Growing an Evangelistic Sunday School*. Nashville: Broadman Press, 1989.

Henderson, David W. *How Will They Hear If We Don't Listen*. Nashville: Broadman-Holman, 1994.

Henry, S. *George Whitfield*. New York: Abingdon Press, 1957.

Hewitt, Hugh. *The Embarrassed Believer: Reviving Christian Witness in an Age of Unbelief*. Nashville: Word Publishing, 1998.

Hill, Junior. *They Call Him Junior: The Autobiography of Junior Hill*. Hartselle, AL: JHI Publishers, 2006.

Hiltner, Seward. *How to Make an Evangelistic Call*. New York: Federal Council of Churches of Christ in America, 1946.

Holcomb, W. *Sam Jones*. New York: Methodist Publishing House, 1947.

Horton, Michael. *The Gospel Commission*. Grand Rapids: Baker, 2011.

Innes, Dick. *I Hate Witnessing*. Ventura, CA: Vision House, 1983.

Hunter, George G. *How to Reach Secular People*. Nashville: Abingdon Press, 1992.

Johnston, E. A. *George Whitefield: A Definitive Biography*. 2 Vols. Stoke-on-Trent, United Kingdom: Tentmaker Publications, 2008.

Johnston, Thomas P. *Charts for a Theology of Evangelism*. Nashville: B&H Academic, 2007.

Jones, Laura. *The Life and Sayings of Sam P. Jones*. Atlanta: Franklin Turner Co., 1907.

Jones, Sam. *Late Sermons: Delivered by the Great Preacher: In His Revival Work. Together with a Biography of Mr. Jones and his Co-Laborer Sam. Small— "Old Si."* Chicago: Rhodes & McClure Publishing Company, 1900.

Jones, Samuel P. *Sam Jones.* New York: Fleming H. Revell Company, 1950.

Jordan, G. Ray. *Faith that Propels.* Nashville: Cokesbury Press, 1935.

Jowett, John H. *The Passion for Souls.* New York: Revell, 1905.

June, Lee, ed. *Evangelism and Discipleship.* Grand Rapids: Zondervan, 1999.

Kantonen, T. A. *Theology of Evangelism.* Philadelphia: Muhlenberg Press, 1954.

Kelley, Jr., Charles S. *Fuel the Fire: Lessons from the History of Southern Baptist Evangelism.* In the series: *A Treasury of Baptist Theology,* edited by Paige Patterson and Jason G. Duesing. Nashville: B & H Academic, 2018.

Kelley, Jr., Charles S. *How Did They Do It? The Story of Southern Baptist Evangelism.* N.p.: Insight Press, 1993.

Kennedy, D. James. *Evangelism Explosion.* Revised by D. James Kennedy and Archie B. Parrish. Foreword by Billy Graham. Wheaton: Tyndale House Publishers, 1977.

Kingsley, Charles W. *Go.* Grand Rapids: Zondervan, 1965.

Kraemer, Hendrik. *A Theology of the Laity.* Philadelphia: The Westminster Press, 1958.

Kramp, John. *Out of Their Faces and into Their Shoes: How to Understand Spiritually Lost People and Give Them Directions to God.* Nashville: Broadman & Holman Publishers, 1995.

Kuiper, Rienk Bouke. *God Centered Evangelism.* Grand Rapids: Baker Book House, 1961.

Larson, David L. *The Evangelism Mandate: Recovering the Centrality of Gospel Preaching.* Grand Rapids: Kregel Publications, 1992.

Leavell, Roland Q. *The Christian's Business*. Nashville: Broadman, 1964.

Leavell, Roland Q. *Evangelism: Christ's Imperative Commission*. Nashville: Broadman Press, 1951.

Leavell, Roland Q., ed. *Preaching the Doctrines of Grace: A Compilation of Evangelistic Sermons by Sixteen Well known Baptist Preachers to Help Promote the Spirit of Soul Winning*. Nashville: Broadman Press, 1939.

Leavell, Roland Q. *The Romance of Evangelism*. Nashville: Sunday School Board of the Southern Baptist Convention, n.d.

Leavell, Roland Q. *Winning Others to Christ*. Nashville: Sunday School Board of the Southern Baptist Convention, 1936.

Lewis, Larry L. *Organize to Evangelize*. Nashville: Broadman Press, 1988.

Little, Paul. *How to Give Away Your Faith*. Chicago: Bible Institute Press, 1938.

Lorimer, G. *Charles Haddon Spurgeon*. Boston: J. H. Earle, 1892.

Ludwig, C. *Sankey Still Sings*. Anderson, IN: Warner Press, 1947.

Macaulay, J. C. and Robert H. Belton. *Personal Evangelism*. Chicago, Moody Press, 1956.

Matthews, C. E. *Every Christian's Job*. Nashville: Broadman Press, 1951.

McDowell, Josh. *The Last Christian Generation*. Holiday, FL: Green Key Books, 2006.

McGavran, Donald. *Understanding Church Growth*. Grand Rapids: Wm. B. Eerdmans, 1980.

McGiffert, A. C. *Jonathan Edwards*. New York: Harper and Brothers, 1942.

McGrath, Alister E. *Explaining Your Faith Without Losing Your Friends*. Grand Rapids: Academy Books, 1989.

McIlrain, Terry. *The New Connection: A Resource for Street Evangelism*. Nashville: Convention Press, 1987.

McRainey, Will. *The Art of Personal Evangelism*. Nashville: Broadman and Holman, 2003.

Miller, Basil. *Charles G. Finney: He Prayed Down Revivals*. Grand Rapids: Zondervan, 1941.

Miller, Basil. *Ten Famous Evangelists*. Grand Rapids: Zondervan, 1949.

Misselbrook, L. R. *Winning the People for Christ*. London: Christian Literature Crusade, n.d.

Moody, P. D. *My Father: An Intimate Portrait of Dwight L. Moody*. Boston: Little, Brown and Company, 1938.

Moody, William. *The Life of Dwight L. Moody*. New York: Fleming H. Revell Company, 1900.

Moore, Waylon. *New Testament Follow-Up for Pastors and Laymen*. Grand Rapids: Eerdmans, 1963.

Morgan, G. Campbell. *Evangelism*. New York: Fleming H. Revell Co., 1904.

Morganthaler, Sally. *Worship Evangelism: Inviting Believers into the Presence of God*. Grand Rapids: Zondervan Publishing House, 1995.

Mueller, Charles S. *The Strategy of Evangelism*. St. Louis: Concordia, 1965.

Mullins, E. Y. *Talks on Soul Winning*. Nashville: Sunday School Board, Southern Baptist Convention, 1920.

Muncy, W. L., Jr. *The History of Evangelism in the United States*. Kansas City: Central Seminary Press, 1945.

Muncy, W. L. Jr. *New Testament Evangelism for Today*. Kansas City, KS: Central Seminary Press, 1941.

Needham, G. *The Life and Labors of Charles H. Spurgeon*. Boston: D. L. Guernsey, 1881.

Neighbor, Jr., Ralph W. *Survival Kit for New Christians: A Practical Guide to Spiritual Growth*. Nashville: Convention Press, 1979.

O'Conner, Elizabeth. *Call to Commitment*. New York: Harper and Row, 1963.

Odle, Joe T. *Church Member's Handbook*. Revised Edition. Nashville: Broadman & Holman Publishers, 1962.

Olford, Stephen. *Successful Soul-Winning*. London: Marshall, Morgen, and Scott, 1958.

Olford, Stephen F. *The Secret of Soul Winning*. Chicago: Moody Press, 1963.

Ottman, F. C. *Wilbur Chapman, a Biography*. Garden City: Doubleday, Page and Co., 1920.

Packer, J. I. *Evangelism and the Sovereignty of God*. London: Inter-Varsity Press, 1961.

Palau, Luis and Timothy Robnett. *Telling the Story*. Ventura, CA: Regal, 2006.

Pell, Edward. *Dwight L. Moody*. Richmond: Johnson, 1900.

Pike, G. *The Life and Work of Charles Haddon Spurgeon*. London: Cassell and Company, n.d.

Pippert, Rebecca Manley. *Out of the Salt Shaker and into the World: Evangelism as a Way of Life*. 20th Anniversary Edition Revised and Expanded. Downers Grove, IL: InterVarsity Press, 1999.

Plummer, Robert L. and John Mark Terry, eds. *Paul's Missionary Methods: In His Time and Ours*. Nottingham, England: Inter-Varsity Press, 2012.

Pollard, Nick. *Evangelism made Slightly Less Difficult: How to Interest People Who Aren't Interested*. Downers Grove, IL: InterVarsity Press, 1997.

Pollock, John. *Billy Graham*. New York: McGraw-Hill, 1966.

Pollock, John. *Moody*. Grand Rapids: Zondervan, 1963.

Posterski, Donald C. *Reinventing Evangelism.* Downers Grove, IL: Intervarsity Press, 1989.

Powell, Ivor. *Don't Lose That Fish.* London: Marshall, Morgan and Scott, 1991.

Ratz, Calvin, Frank Tillapaugh, and Myron Augsberger. *Mastering Outreach and Evangelism.* N.p.: Multnomah, 1990.

Queen, Matt. *Everyday Evangelism.* Fort Worth, TX: Seminary Hill Press, 2015.

Rainer, Thom. *Effective Evangelistic Churches: Successful Churches Reveal What Works and What Doesn't.* Nashville: Broadman and Holman Publishers, 1996.

Reid, Alvin. *Evangelism Handbook: Biblical, Spiritual, Intentional, Missional.* Foreword by Thom S. Rainer. Afterword by Roy Fish. Nashville: B & H Academic, 2009.

Reid, Alvin. *Introduction to Evangelism.* Nashville: Broadman & Holman Publishers, 1998.

Reid, Alvin. *Sharing Jesus {without freaking out}: Evangelism the Way You Were Born to Do It.* Nashville: B & H Academic, 2017.

Rice, John R. *The Soul-Winner's Fire.* Chicago: Moody Press, 1941.

Richardson, Rick. *Evangelism Outside the Box.* Downers Grove, IL: Intervarsity Press, 2000.

Robertson, A. T. *Jesus as a Soul-Winner: And Other Sermons.* New York: Fleming H. Revell Company, 1937.

Robinson, Darrell W. *Incredibly Gifted: A Fresh, Biblical Look at Spiritual Gifts.* Garland, TX: Hannibal Books, 2002.

Robinson, Darrell W. *People Sharing Jesus.* Nashville: Thomas Nelson Publishers, 1995.

Robinson, Darrell W. *Total Church Life: How to Be a First Century Church in a 21st Century World.* Foreword by Billy Graham. Nashville: Broadman & Holman Publishers, 1997.

Rodeheaver, H. *Twenty Years With Billy Sunday.* Nashville: Cokesbury Press, 1936.

Rogers, Adrian. *Preaching for a Verdict.* Session X from the Series *What Every Pastor Ought to Know* by Adrian Rogers. Memphis, TN: Love Worth Finding (https://www.lwf.org).

Salter, Darius. *American Evangelism: Its Theology and Practice.* Grand Rapids: Baker Books, 1996.

Sanders, Oswald. *The Divine Art of Soul-Winning.* Chicago: Moody Press, n.d.

Sanderson, Leonard. *Personal Soul-Winning.* Nashville: Convention Press, 1958.

Sangster, William. *Let Me Commend.* New York: Abingdon-Cokesbury Press, 1948.

Scarborough, Lee Rutland. *Endued to Win.* Nashville: Sunday School Board of the Southern Baptist Convention, 1922.

Scarborough, L. R. *Holy Places and Precious Promises.* Nashville: Sunday School Board of the Southern Baptist Convention, 1924.

Scarborough, L. R. *How Jesus Won Men.* Grand Rapids: Baker Book House, 1972.

Scarborough, L. R. *With Christ after the Lost: A Search for Souls.* Revised and Expanded by E. D. Head. Nashville: Broadman Press, 1952.

Scharpff, Paulus. *History of Evangelism: Three Hundred Years of Evangelism in Germany, Great Britain, and the United States of America.* Translated by Helga Bender Henry. Grand Rapids: William B. Eerdmans Publishing Company, 1966.

Shipman, Mike. *Any-3: Anyone, Anywhere, Any Time: Win Muslims to Christ Now.* Monument, CO: WIGTake Resources, 2013.

Shoemaker, Samuel. *With the Holy Spirit and With Fire*. New York: Harper, 1960.

Simpson, Michael L. *Permission Evangelism: When to Talk When to Walk*. Colorado Springs, CO: NexGen, 2003.

Skreslet, Stanley. *Picturing Christian Witness*. Grand Rapids: Eerdmans, 2006.

Smith, Bailey E. *Real Evangelism: Exposing the Subtle Substitutes*. Nashville: Word Publishing, 1999.

Smith, Gypsy. *Gypsy Smith, His Life and Work*. New York: Fleming H. Revell Co., 1902.

Smith, Oswald. *The Consuming Fire*. Grand Rapids: Zondervan, 1954.

Smith Oswald. *The Passion for Souls*. London: Marshall, Morgan and Scott, 1950.

Spurgeon, C. H. *The Autobiography of Charles H. Spurgeon*. Philadelphia: American Baptist Publications Co., n.d.

Spurgeon, Charles H. *The Soul Winner*. Condensed and Edited by David Otis Fuller. Grand Rapids: Zondervan Publishing House, 1948.

Stetzer, Ed and David Putman. *Breaking the Missional Code: Your Church Can Become a Missionary in Your Community*. Nashville: B & H Publishing Group, 2006.

Stott, John R. W. *Basic Christianity*. Grand Rapids: Wm. B. Eerdmans Publishing Co., 1958.

Strachan, Kenneth. *Evangelism in Depth*. Chicago: Moody Press, 1961.

Street, R. Alan. *The Effective Invitation: A Practical Guide for the Pastor*. Grand Rapids: Kregel Publications, 1984.

Strobel, Lee. *The Case for Faith*. Grand Rapids: Zondervan, 2000.

Sweazey, George E. *Effective Evangelism: The Greatest Work in the World*. New York: Harper & Brothers, 1953.

Tarn, Stanley. *Every Christian a Soul-Winner*. Nashville: Thomas Nelson, 1975.

Taylor, Vincent. *Doctrine and Evangelism*. London: The Epworth Press, 1953.

Terry, John Mark. *Church Evangelism: Creating a Culture for Growth in Your Congregation*. Nashville: Broadman & Holman Publishers, 1997.

Terry, John Mark and Robert L. Gallagher. *Encountering the History of Missions from the Early Church to Today*. In the series Encountering Mission. Edited by A. Scott Moreau. Grand Rapids: Baker Academic, 2017.

Terry, John Mark. *Evangelism: A Concise History*. Nashville: Broadman & Holman Publishers, 1994.

Thomas, J. V. *Investing in Eternity: The Indigenous Satellite Church Strategy: A Practical Guide to Multi-Church Planting*. Foreword by Charles L. Chaney. N.p.: 1991.

Thompson, W. Oscar. *Concentric Circles of Concern*. Nashville: Broadman Press, 1981.

Tidsworth, Floyd. *Life Cycle of a New Congregation*. Foreword by Charles L. Chaney. Nashville: Broadman Press, 1992.

Torrey, Reuben A. *Personal Work*. New York: Revell, 1901.

Torrey, Reuben A. *Why God Used D. L. Moody*. Chicago: Moody Press, 1947.

Trotman, Dawson. *Born to Reproduce*. N.p. Back to the Bible, 1957.

Trueblood, David E. *Company of the Committed*. New York: Harper and Brothers, 1961.

Trueblood, David E. *Your Other Vocation*. New York: Harper and Brothers, 1952.

Truett, George W. *A Quest for Souls: Comprising All the Sermons Preached and Prayer Offered in a Series of Gospel Meetings Held in Fort Worth, Texas.* Nashville: Broadman Press, 1917.

Trumbull, Charles G. *Taking Men Alive.* New York: New York: Revell, 1920.

Turner, J. Clyde. *Soul-Winning Doctrines.* Nashville: Convention Press, 1943.

Tyerman, L. *The Life of Rev. George Whitefield. New York:* Anson D. F. Randolph and Company, 1877.

Veerman, David R. *Youth Evangelism.* N.p.: Victor Books, 1984.

Wagner, C. Peter. *Your Church Can Grow: Seven Vital Signs of a Healthy Church.* Ventura, CA: Regal Books, 1984.

Walker, Alan. *The Whole Gospel for the Whole World.* New York: Abingdon, 1957.

Wayland, Herman L. *Charles H. Spurgeon.* Philadelphia: American Baptist Publications Company, 1892.

Webber, Robert E. *Ancient-Future Evangelism.* Grand Rapids: Baker, 2003.

Welch, Bobby H. *Evangelism through the Sunday School: A Journey of FAITH.* Nashville: LifeWay Press, 1997.

Wilson, Geo. M, ed. *Evangelism Now: U. S. Congress on Evangelism— Minneapolis, Minnesota 1969.* In *Official Reference Volume: Papers and Reports.* Minneapolis: World Wide Publications, 1970.

Wood, A. Skevington. *Evangelism: Its Theology and Practice.* Grand Rapids: Zondervan, 1966.

ENDNOTES

1   Much of the information in this section comes from James A. Patterson's excellent book, *To All the World: A History of Mid-America Baptist Theological Seminary, 1972–1997* (Memphis, TN: Mid-America Baptist Theological Seminary, 1997). For more information on the early life and wartime experiences of Gray Allison, see also: *Sons of the 43rd: The Story of Delmar Dotson, Gray Allison, and the Men of the 43rd Bombardment Group in the Southwest Pacific* by Michael R. Spradlin (Memphis, TN: Innovo Publishing, 2016).

2   An excellent resource for this topic is the book by T. V. Farris, *Mighty to Save: A Study in Old Testament Soteriology* (Nashville: Broadman Press, 1993).

3   Jim R. Sibley. At the time of the lecture, Dr. Sibley was a faculty member of the Criswell College of Dallas, Texas. I have never found his work in print so that I can give him a proper citation, but I believe his cultural interpretation of the Acts 1:8 passage has significant merit, and I have included the information in this work.

4   C. E. Autrey, *You Can Win Souls* (Nashville: Broadman Press, 1961), p. 2.

5   Allison Note: "I am indebted to Richard C. H. Lenski, *The Interpretation of St. Luke's Gospel,* and to William Manson, *The Gospel of Luke,* for ideas here."

6   William Manson, *The Gospel of Luke* (London: Hodder, 1948).

7   J. B. Phillips, *Letters to Young Churches* (London: Macmillan, 1955).

8   W. H. Auden, "September 1939," quoted by Norman Pittenger, *Christ in the Haunted Wood* (n.p.: Seabury Press, 1953).

9   Robert Luccock, *If God Be for Us: Sermons on the Gifts of the Gospel* (New York: Harper, 1954).

10   David MacLennan, *Entrusted With the Gospel* (Philadelphia: Westminster Press, 1956).

11   Elizabeth Barrett Browning, *Aurora Leigh, Second Book.* https://www.poetryfoundation.org/poems/145568/aurora-leigh-second-book.

[12]   George E. Sweazey, *Effective Evangelism: The Greatest Work in the World* (New York: HarperCollins Publishers, 1976), p. 37.

[13]   Mark Noll, Nathan O. Hatch, George M. Marsden, David F. Wells, and John D. Woodbridge, eds. *Eerdmans' Handbook to Christianity in America* (Grand Rapids: William B. Eerdmans Publishing Company, 1983), pp. 381-382.

[14]   Quoted by Missionary May Perry in chapel at New Orleans Baptist Theological Seminary, December 3, 1953. Personal notes of B. Gray Allison.

[15]   Winston Crawley, "Know Your Baptist Missions," *The Orient*, 1962 ed.

[16]   John Oxenham, *Bees in Amber: A Little Book of Thoughtful Verse* (n.p.: n.p., 1913), p. 80.

[17]   Billy Graham, *Baptist Standard*, November 21, 1962.

[18]   J. B. Phillips, *The Church Under the Cross* (n.p.: The Highway Press, 1956), p. 80.

[19]   David Adeney, *The Unchanging Commission* (Downers Grove, IL: Inter-Varsity Press, 1956), pp. 76, 77.

[20]   Eugene Harrison, *How to Win Souls: A Manual of Personal Evangelism* (n.p.: Van Kampen Press, 1952), p. 140.

[21]   Louis Evans, *Life's Hidden Power* (n.p.: Marshal, M & S, 1959), pp. 35, 36.

[22]   The four-fold idea, in different words, is set forth in L. R. Scarborough, *With Christ After the Lost*, and in Eugene L. Harrison, *How to Win Souls*.

[23]   Edward Gibbon, *The Decline and Fall of the Roman Empire*, V. (Boston: Phillips, 1856), 6 volumes.

[24]   William Temple, *Basic Christianity*, pp. 66-67. Editor's Note: I am unable to find which of the many William Temple writings Dr. Allison refers to here. You can see: William Temple, *The Works of William Temple, Bart., Complete in 4 Vol. To Which Is Prefixed, the Life and Character of the Author, Considerable Enlarged.*

[25]   William Temple, *Basic Christianity*, pp. 66-67.

[26]   Ibid., p. 67.

[27]   Halford Luccock, *Marching Off the Map* (New York: Harper & Brothers, 1952), pp. 136-137.

28   Henry Cook, *The Theology of Evangelism* (London: Carey Kingsport Press, 1951).

29   John Wesley, *Twelve Rules*. John Wesley had voluminous writings that have been quoted in numerous sources. The exact source that Gray Allison used here was not listed in his notes.

30   Richard Baxter, no citation was given in B. Gray Allison's notes.

31   No citation for this quote was given in B. Gray Allison's notes.

32   George Sweazey, *Effective Evangelism: The Greatest Work in the World* (New York: HarperCollins Publishers, 1976), p. 56.

33   Gerald Kennedy, *A Reader's Notebook: An Anthology of Illustrations for Preachers & Other Public Speaker, Drawn from a Variety of Sources, both Classic & Contemporary* (New York: Harper & Brothers, 1953), p. 8.

34   Carrie E. Beck and Chas. H. Gabriel, "Nobody Told Me of Jesus," in *Enduring Hymns* (https://hymnary.org/hymn/PCSS1916/page/80), n.p.

35   Gray B. [sic] Allison, "Person to Person" in *Royal Service Magazine* vol. 60, no. 7 (Birmingham: Woman's Missionary Union of the Southern Baptist Convention, 1966), n.p.

36   Joe T. Odle, *Church Member's Handbook*. Rev. ed. (Nashville: Broadman & Holman Publishers, 1962), p. 7.

37   Bill Bright, *Have You Heard of the Four Spiritual Laws?* CRU and Bright Media Foundation, Inc., 2003–2018.

38   See *https://e3partners.org/training/* for a full explanation of their means and methods.

39   See *https://evangelismexplosion.org* for a full explanation of their means and methods.

40   The end of this chapter contains all works cited within the article.

41   This explanation and example come from someone who works in a Muslim setting and has extensive experience in sharing the gospel with Muslims. Though I cannot give a full citation for security reasons, I am grateful for the information and the work of this person.

[42]   Mike Shipman, *Any-3: Anyone, Anywhere, and Any Time: Win Muslims to Christ Now* (Monument CO: WIGTake Resources, 2013).

[43]   Adrian Rogers, *Preaching for a Verdict*. From Session X of the series *What Every Pastor Ought* to Know (Memphis, TN: Love Worth Finding (https://www.lwf.org), n.d.), p. 6.

[44]   McGavran, Donald A. *Understanding Church Growth*. Third Edition. Revised and Edited by C. Peter Wagner (Grand Rapids: William B. Eerdmans Publishing Company), pp. 71-72.

[45]   This section is a summation of the editor's interview with Dr. Brad Roderick. Dr. Roderick has over thirty years of missions experience. He and his wife, Gretchen, served eleven years with the North American Mission Board and nineteen years with the International Mission Board, both of the Southern Baptist Convention. After retiring from the International Mission Board, Dr. Roderick served as a professor of missions at Mid-America Baptist Theological Seminary.

[46]   Roderick, interview with the editor.

[47]   Robinson, Darrell W., *Total Church Life: How to Be a First Century Church in a 21st Century World* (Nashville: Broadman & Holman Publishers, 1997), pp. 1-9.

[48]   Dayton, Edward K. and David A Fraser, *Planning Strategies for World Evangelization* (Grand Rapids: Eerdmans, 1990), pp.viii-xii.

[49]   L. R. Scarborough, *With Christ After the Lost: A Search for Souls*. revised and expanded by E. D. Head (Nashville: Broadman Press, 1952).

[50]   Flake, Arthur, *Building a Standard Sunday School*. Reprint 1959 (Nashville: Convention Press, 1959).

[51]   https://statisticalatlas.com/United-States/Overview. The information from Thomas Hammond is based on a series of interviews of Thomas Hamond with the editor of this work. The material has previously been unpublished but is based on Hammond's decades of experience doing evangelism in local churches, at state convention level, and as a part of the North American Mission Board of the Southern Baptist Convention.